GOSPEL *hope in* GRIEF & LOSS

KRISTYN PEREZ

004   **WHAT IS GRIEF?**
The Definition of Grief, A Word on Triggers, Types of Grief

012   **WHY IS THERE GRIEF?**
The Fall, Loss

018   **PHYSICAL RESPONSES TO GRIEF**
Shock and Denial, Sleeplessness, Short-term Memory Loss, Escapism and Addictions, Changes in Identity, Trouble Concentrating and Making Decisions, Body Pain or Sickness

042   **EMOTIONAL RESPONSES TO GRIEF**
Sadness, Bargaining, Loneliness, Guilt, Shame, and Regret, Suicidal Thoughts, Apathy, Anger, Envy, Relief, Anxiety

086   **SPIRITUAL RESPONSES TO GRIEF**
Anger at God, Despair at Living, When God Feels Distant, Purposelessness in Life, Doubt in the Lord's Goodness, Hope in the Lord

106   **HOW TO GRIEVE**
Acknowledge Your Loss, Cry Out to the Lord, Be Honest with Your Emotions, Understand Your Story, Grieve with Hope, Identify New Goals, Plan for Special Events, Remembering Your Loved Ones, Find Community, Cling to Scripture

160   **HELPING SOMEONE WHO IS GRIEVING**
Listen, Pray, The Ministry of Presence, Acts of Service, Be Patient, Consistent, and Loving

180   **GOD IN OUR GRIEF**
He is with Us, He Weeps with Us, He Redeems Your Suffering

192   **THE FUTURE OF GRIEF**

01

WHAT IS GRIEF?

The Definition of Grief
A Word on Triggers
Types of Grief

THE DEFINITION OF GRIEF

Grief is a deep sorrow of the soul and is often as a result of a loss. It is not linear or predictable. It does not follow any rules. It is slow and rarely conforms to our timelines. It can come in waves, leaving us breathless and quickly sweeping over our hearts in an unexpected instant. Or, it can linger, bringing with it gradual darkness, sadness, and despair. To complicate matters, grief can be experienced by each person in dramatically different ways. For some, it feels like anger, fear, or numbness. For others, it leads them to question everything; they might withdraw in apathy or press into their faith.

Grief brings disruption to every aspect of our lives. Perhaps there is an empty chair at Christmas dinner this year or an empty space in the bed each night. Perhaps a wave of grief comes as we begin to text our loved one but are brutally confronted once again with the sting of their loss. Or maybe, you grieve what could have been —what *should* have been. You grieve each time a co-worker brags about her successful children while remembering your own child who is bound by the chains of addiction. You feel a pierce of pain as you watch an older couple stroll gingerly through the park, recalling that your dreams of marital bliss were replaced by divorce attorneys and affair allegations.

> GRIEF CAN BE EXPERIENCED BY EACH PERSON IN *dramatically different ways*

This booklet will not be an instant fix as we explore grief and the gospel in the following pages. There are no quick, trite answers that will erase the pain of grief. There are no words that will bring enough meaning to justify your loss. We will not try to "fix you." Instead, we will ponder grief together, examining the spiritual, emotional, and physical effects of it in our lives. We will discover what Scripture has to say about grief and press into the hope of a good Savior. We will look to God, who is with us in our pain and knows our sorrows. Indeed, He is a faithful friend in joy and in sorrow. He is near to the broken-hearted and acquainted with grief (Psalm 34:18, Isaiah 53:3). He is our very present help in time of need (Psalm 46:1).

A WORD ON TRIGGERS

As we discuss grief, consider your specific triggers. Certain phrases, examples, or topics in this booklet may be extremely raw for you. Read this booklet slowly, pausing to digest its material at your own pace. It may be helpful to share this with a friend, highlighting the sections that you identify with, which can help provide language to describe your pain.

Similarly, use this as an opportunity to reflect on the triggers in your daily life that make grief even harder. These may include special occasions, birthdays, anniversaries, or family traditions. Triggers also include things like a location that is difficult to visit or a particular season or smell. As you identify these triggers, write them down to refer back to later. Moments of intense, unexpected grief are sometimes referred to as "grief spasms." When these occur, try to deal with them as soon as possible. When we ignore or discount our grief, we save it for a later, often more severe, buildup and possible breakdown.

Triggers due to loss can often result from predictable events. If you have trauma due to an unexpected accident, you may dread the sound of the phone ringing. Or, if you have recently experienced the loss of a child, the mention of Mother's Day may bring you to tears. As much as possible, make plans for key events ahead of time. Think about what you want to do for holidays, parties, and gifts. Write, talk, and process through your feelings surrounding these events. What bothers you about them? What do you fear or dread? Let others know that this will be a hard day for you. Consider changing your traditions or making new ones that honor your loss or loved one.

> "
> WHEN WE IGNORE OR DISCOUNT OUR GRIEF, WE SAVE IT FOR A LATER, OFTEN MORE SEVERE, BUILDUP AND *possible breakdown*.

TYPES OF GRIEF

Grief comes in many forms. We may grieve a recent job loss or a divorce. We can grieve a breakup, loss of a dream, or loss of innocence due to abuse. Or we may experience grief due to the loss of a loved one. Indeed, anything we love, we can lose. And grief is a natural response to loss.

Many heroes of our faith also experienced grief. Isaac and Rebekah grieved the decisions of their son (Genesis 26:35). Job grieved

greatly when he lost his children, property, and livestock (Job 2:13). Even Jesus grieved the loss of His friend, Lazarus, though He knew that He would bring him to life moments later (John 11:35). Similarly, the Spirit Himself can be grieved by our rebellion against God (Ephesians 4:30). Grief can result from many disappointments, such as disaster, death, and disobedience.

While there are many types and forms of grief, we must be careful not to compare or rank them. We should not discount someone's grief because it is not "as bad as it could have been" or because "others have gone through worse." In the same way, we cannot assume to understand another's grief because each person's grief is unique. Two people may experience the same loss in dramatically different ways, based on their background, personality, or closeness to the person. The way we process grief can vary based on factors such as how we heard about the loss, our view of death, or the suddenness of the loss. For the loss of a loved one, our grief processing will vary depending on factors such as the closeness of the relationship, who found them, and if there was a body. The many causes of grief require us to continue our grief journey with gentleness, grace, and reliance on the Holy Spirit.

> **"**
> WHILE THERE ARE MANY TYPES
> AND FORMS OF GRIEF,
> *we must be careful*
> NOT TO COMPARE OR RANK THEM.

02

WHY IS THERE GRIEF?

The Fall
Loss

THE FALL

The first question that comes to mind in grief is often, *"Why?"* *Why is this happening? Why did they have to die? Why do I feel so alone? Why did this happen? Why God?* We may think that we did something to cause this pain. Maybe we think we can do something to keep it from happening again. As we discover in grief, so much of life is beyond our control, including our sufferings.

In Scripture, the "why" of grief can be traced back to the fall in Genesis 3. When God made the world, He created everything good. He designed the sun and the stars, the moon, and the animals and said they were good. He also made Adam and Eve and placed them in the garden to have authority over the land and subdue it. He gave them important work to do by day and walked with them at night. He also gave them this command: Do not eat of the fruit of the Tree of the Knowledge of Good and Evil. Unfortunately, Adam and Eve did not obey this command. This event in biblical history is called the fall.

As a result of the fall, brokenness was introduced into every area of our lives, from our bodies to our minds to our spirits. Because of the fall, we get sick, anxious, and experience despair. We feel far from God and wonder where He is. We experience trials and tests of our faith. We endure a lifetime of suffering until one day we will also die and meet our Maker face to face. On this day, He will come again to make all things new. He will wipe every tear and right every wrong. He will make all things good again. Until that day, we remain, hoping for the future redemption of our bodies. We grieve, knowing that death is the last and final enemy (1 Corinthians 15:26). We mourn, agreeing with God that it was never meant to be this way. We look to Christ, who is with us in our pain and weeps with us.

LOSS

Grief accompanies loss. We grieve because we have lost someone or something that we love. We ache because sin, brokenness, death, and disease ravish the world. Our loved one is gone, and we protest their loss. We protest their loss because our love for that person perseveres.

Unfortunately, if we live long enough, we will all experience grief at one time or another. And usually, one loss is accompanied by a series of other losses. If we lose a loved one, for example, we are faced with the reality our loved one is gone and the loss of future dreams. Holidays, vacations, and everyday moments suddenly look very different than we expected. Or perhaps, with the loss of a loved one, our entire identities suddenly change. We are no longer a wife but a widow. Grief feels like a consuming hole of destruction, with no part of life left unaffected.

When facing a loss such as the death of a loved one, the finality of our loss can be devastating. It can blindside us and leave us disoriented or unprepared to face tomorrow. That all said, it is normal and healthy to grieve the losses of life.

> *it is normal and healthy*
> TO GRIEVE THE LOSSES OF LIFE

03

PHYSICAL RESPONSES TO GRIEF

Shock and Denial
Sleeplessness
Short-term Memory Loss
Escapism and Addictions
Changes in Identity
Trouble Concentrating and Making Decisions
Body Pain or Sickness

SHOCK AND DENIAL

The first stage of grief is usually shock. You may feel stuck in a dreamlike state, disassociated from the present. You cannot think clearly and feel like your brain is in a fog. The reality of your loss has not yet sunk in. Your last memory with your loved one may seem as vivid as though it was currently happening. You may even wonder if you are going crazy.

The numbness of shock or the inability to fully understand what is happening is natural. Shock is actually a God-given instinct of protection for you. When you experience loss, it takes time to adjust to your new reality. The experience of shock will fade with time, during which, we have the opportunity to confront our grief head-on or to continue down into a path of denial. Similar to shock, denial is a coping mechanism of refusing to recognize reality. You may refer to your loved one in the present tense or think that you saw your loved one in a crowd. Although denial is a natural response to loss, we must eventually accept reality and confront our pain. Continuing to live in denial does not mean that our grief will disappear. Instead, it will spill out into other areas of life. Only as we acknowledge our pain can we begin to find healing for our grief.

Even as we experience shock or denial at our loss, we can have comfort knowing that nothing takes God by surprise. He is not caught off guard at our loss or in denial at their occurrence. He knows all and is actively sustaining you through them. As Psalm 46:1 says, "God is our refuge and strength, a helper who is always found in times of trouble." God is our strength and our safe place, who promises to uphold you in even the deepest of trials. Though the present reality may seem distant or impossible to grasp, God never is. He is our very present help in time of need. Even when we cannot recognize reality or feel unprepared to face tomorrow, God will continue to hold our world together.

A Prayer for One in Shock or Denial

Lord, I cannot believe what has just happened. Never in a million years did I expect this heartbreaking loss. I'm at a loss for words. I'm in shock. It doesn't feel real. And yet, You were not surprised by this terrible situation. Even when I feel like I cannot face tomorrow, I know that You will be there. My eternal hope is secure in You. May that bring me comfort today.

God, please help me to process this new reality. It feels like the ground was pulled out from under me, but You are my rock. Help me to face this loss head-on, knowing that You are with me. You are my Shepherd and the One who holds me when I fall. Let me find peace and comfort in Your promises. Help me today and every tomorrow, I pray. I cannot do this alone.

Amen.

SLEEPLESSNESS

You glance at the clock; it is 3:00 AM. Another night awake. You try to close your eyes and rest but cannot find the sweet relief of sleep. In your exhaustion, you turn to the TV again, watching for hours on end but unable to truly rest. Or maybe nightmares haunt your sleep, invading the vulnerability of unconscious thoughts. You wake as your mind replays the loss over and over. Anxiety flies in, an unwelcome but familiar friend — your fear and panic peak in the quietness of the night.

Sleeplessness is a common physical response to grief and one that is common within the pages of Scripture. After losing his health, property, and family, Job said, "When I lie down I think, 'When will I get up?' But the evening drags on endlessly, and I toss and turn until dawn" (Job 7:4). Similarly, the Apostle Paul endured sleepless nights as he endured sorrow upon sorrow (2 Corinthians 6:4-5). It seems that they could not escape their trials, even through sleep.

Nighttime can become a battleground for our thoughts as we let our guard down in exhaustion. When we are tired and worn out in grief, we are tempted to doubt God's goodness and wonder how we will make it through tomorrow. While this temptation is normal, we are not powerless in it. We have a Great High Priest, a mediator who intercedes to God on our behalf, even when we do not have the words to pray (Hebrews 7:25). If you know that nighttime is a challenge for you, make a plan. Pick out verses you will recite and memorize in the night, such as Psalm 23. Pray to the Lord, expressing all of your concerns to the Lord. As the psalmist says, "When I think of you as I lie on my bed, I meditate on you during the night watches" (Psalm 63:6).

Even if the world around us sleeps, our God never does (Psalm 121:4). His Word strengthens us for each battle. He is always awake, always interceding for us, always protecting us. He is near, even in the middle of the night.

A Prayer for the Sleepless Night

Lord, I turn to You tonight as sleep evades me and my mind runs wild. I just want to rest. I want a few minutes of relief, and I remember a time when sleep felt easy. But now, I cannot relax, even in my exhaustion. Yet, even still, I know that You are enough for me. You are my God. Even when I cannot think clearly or when darkness surrounds me, You are here. Even in my darkest moments, You hold my world together.

Lord, will You help me rest tonight? As I lay awake on my bed tonight, will You bring Scripture to mind and help me meditate on what is true? Even when I cannot sleep, I know that You are listening because You, too, never sleep. You are always listening, always watching, always protecting. Help me to have the energy to face the day tomorrow and entrust my future into Your hands. Help me to sleep, knowing you are covering me in Your loving protection.

Amen.

SHORT-TERM MEMORY LOSS

Short-term memory loss is another common symptom of grief. You cannot find your keys again. You cannot remember simple instructions, directions, or people's names. You might have trouble making simple decisions that accompany your grief, including funeral details. You may have trouble remembering stories that do not include your loved one. Time may feel distorted, either racing impossibly or slow as a snail. As you continue in your grief journey, it is normal for your memory to be affected. If you experience this grief symptom, have patience with yourself. Your body has undergone great stress, and forgetfulness is a normal biological response.

Until your memory returns, establish a system that can help you in the day-to-day. Keep a calendar, and set alarms to help you remember when you need to be somewhere. Jot down memories of your loved one if you are afraid you will forget them. Also, seek help from those around you. Ask for help and reminders from friends or family about key appointments or commitments. As much as possible, try to postpone decisions you need to make surrounding your grief, including your living arrangements.

Even when we cannot remember details clearly, we have confidence that God never forgets anything. He is never lost, confused, or disoriented. God is the holder of all the memories of the world, and He will never forget your loved one. We can cling to Him when our world feels confusing and disruptive because He is our rock. He holds every one of our tears in a bottle, and He knows what we forget. God will help you get through this season. He knows all, and He cares for us. He will help us even in the midst of short-term memory loss.

> EVEN WHEN WE CANNOT
> REMEMBER DETAILS CLEARLY,
> WE HAVE CONFIDENCE THAT
> *God never forgets anything*

Tools to Help with Short-term Memory Loss

If you are struggling with short-term memory loss, consider implementing strategies that can help you in your day-to-day:

1. **PRAY.**
   Ask God to help you remember any important details for your day.
2. **KEEP A CALENDAR.**
   Write down even small details that you need to remember.
3. **TAKE CARE OF YOUR BODY.**
   Take vitamins, exercise, and try to sleep regular hours.
4. **POSTPONE IMPORTANT DECISIONS IF YOU CAN.**
5. **ASK FRIENDS AND FAMILY FOR HELP.**
   Ask that they would call and remind you of appointments and commitments.
6. **SET ALARMS FOR KEY APPOINTMENTS.**

ESCAPISM AND ADDICTIONS

Maybe you are not struggling with short-term memory loss. Instead, you *want* to forget. You want to escape the unbearable pain of grief and breathe normally again, even if just for a second. You want the pressing weight on your chest to subside. As you cope with your loss, you find momentary relief in emotional eating or by enjoying one glass of wine and then another. Or maybe you turn on the TV and escape into first one movie and then another. Before you know it, the bottle is gone, and you have binged the entire TV series. One night of escape turns into another and then another. Suddenly, it has been a week, a month, or a year with the same emotion-numbing behaviors. You begin to wonder, *"Is this a problem? Do I need help?"* If this describes you today, you are not alone. Addiction and escapism are normal temptations for even the holiest of Christians. In our grief, we face uncharted battles daily, in a season when we already feel weak.

Ironically, when we try to numb our grief, it does not make it disappear. It only postpones and extends it. Instead of trying to escape our emotions, we have a better option. We can turn to the One who provides lasting healing and hope in our grief. Turning to God does not mean that you need to process your deepest emotions all at once. Rather, as we press into God's character, we find a God who comforts us in our pain and sustains us in our weakness. He is a patient Father and knows what we can endure. He is our help, our strength, and our hope. He promises to be with us, and He gives us the strength to endure. We do not need to escape from our grief because we know that God is with us in it. We can have the courage to see reality clearly through activities such as those on pages 109-159 because God will sustain us.

If you are struggling with escapist or addictive behaviors, talk to your local pastor or a trusted friend. There is no shame in getting help in a difficult time. God has provided community as a means of help for His people. Press into the biblical means of grace, including the Word, prayer, counseling, and biblical community.

> *God has provided community*
> **AS A MEANS OF HELP FOR HIS PEOPLE**

Identifying Escapism Flowchart

START HERE

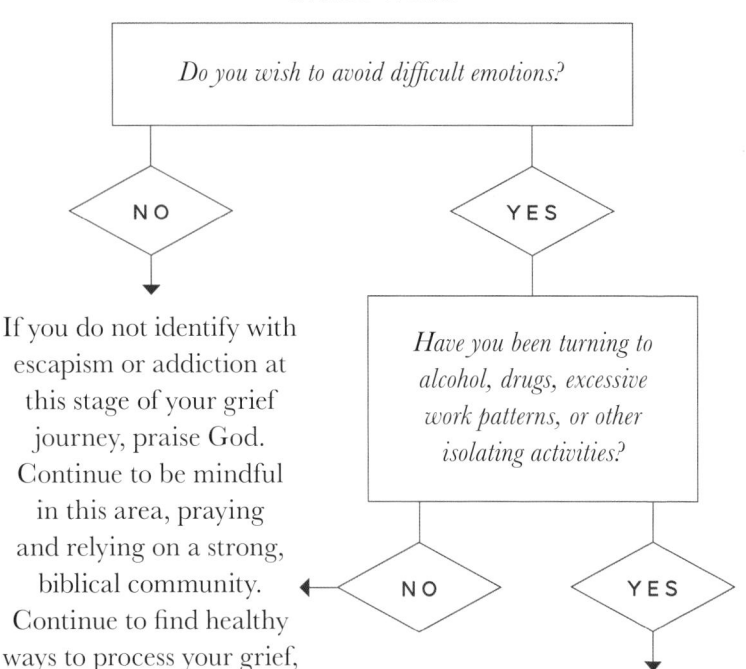

Do you wish to avoid difficult emotions?

NO

If you do not identify with escapism or addiction at this stage of your grief journey, praise God. Continue to be mindful in this area, praying and relying on a strong, biblical community. Continue to find healthy ways to process your grief, including the activities on pages 109-159.

YES

Have you been turning to alcohol, drugs, excessive work patterns, or other isolating activities?

NO

YES

Praise God that He has given you insight into this area of your life. If you have identified addiction or escapism as a problem in your life, talk to someone about it. Meet with your local pastor or a biblical counselor. Confide in a trusted friend or family member. Get help. There is no shame in seeking biblical help in the midst of any kind of addiction, and there is hope waiting for you in His Word. Turn to Him today, confessing your desire to escape this pain and asking for His help as you grieve.

CHANGES IN IDENTITY

When we experience loss, our entire identity may change. Perhaps you have lost your job, and you are no longer an engineer. Maybe you lost your house, and you are no longer a homeowner. Maybe you lost your mother, and you are no longer a child. Or perhaps you have lost a spouse and are no longer a wife but a widow.

A feeling of disorientation often accompanies changes in identity. You may wonder, "Who am I now?" You were someone's aunt or mother or sister, but now that place they filled stands empty. Or maybe your closest friends were couples, and now you feel left out or awkward after your divorce. The loss you have experienced has affected not only your emotions but your very title in life.

We will each go through many changes of status throughout our lifetimes. It is healthy to grieve this loss as we come to understand our new reality. In a broken world, we will lose many things, from jobs to houses to loved ones. Before God, we can mourn this loss without hesitation. As we do so, we can also press into the reality of Scripture, remembering that God's calling of us remains unchanged. As a child of God, our identity in Christ is secure. Nothing can shake our status before Him. We are God's adopted children forever. We are chosen, loved, and accepted forever. We are His friends forever. We are His beloved, and that will never change. When the foundation of your world feels shaky, and your entire identity has changed, cling to the Lord. Let His definition of you comfort you in these unstable times.

Complete the following exercise to remember your secure identity in Christ.

Identity in Christ Exercise

Look up these verses. What does each verse tell you about your identity in Christ?

I PETER 2:9

PHILIPPIANS 3:20

JOHN 15:15

Identity in Christ Exercise

Look up these verses. What does each verse tell you about your identity in Christ?

1 CORINTHIANS 3:16

EPHESIANS 1:4

JOHN 1:12

GALATIANS 4:7

I JOHN 3:1-2

EPHESIANS 1:5

TROUBLE CONCENTRATING AND MAKING DECISIONS

Grief affects our minds. After the great author and Christian apologist C.S. Lewis lost his wife, he described his experience as if there were a blanket between him and the world. He found it hard to listen to what others were saying. Every thought felt disrupted, and he had trouble concentrating. He wrote that it was hard to focus because every thought led to him thinking about the loss of his wife. Thoughts of his late wife quite literally took over his brain. And that is the reality of grief—with grief, our habits, emotions, thought patterns, and future plans all face the reality of our loss.

To complicate matters, many decisions need to be made in grief, including funeral details, financial provisions, or living arrangements. It may be difficult for you to think about the future and make the necessary decisions around loss. As much as possible, defer decisions for a later date. In a haste to move on, you may decide to move to a new house, only to discover in a year that you miss all the memories you had in your old home with your loved one. Give yourself time to grieve and make these decisions at a later date, if possible. When decisions must be made, ask God for wisdom, and seek help from the people around you. Ask for wise counsel in financial decisions and big life adjustments. Then, do not be afraid to make a decision.

When you are having trouble concentrating or making decisions, fill your mind with the stable truths of God's Word. Play the Bible on audio as the backdrop of your day. Write Scripture on note cards to hang around your house. Depend on trusted relationships around you, and create rhythms to fill your mind with what is true, especially when it is hard to dwell on these truths naturally.

Scripture to Meditate On

When you are having trouble concentrating on the present, meditate on God's Word. Consider these sample verses.

PSALM 34:18
The Lord is near the brokenhearted;
he saves those crushed in spirit.

PSALM 46:1
God is our refuge and strength, a helper
who is always found in times of trouble.

REVELATION 21:4
He will wipe away every tear from their
eyes. Death will be no more; grief, crying,
and pain will be no more, because the
previous things have passed away.

PSALM 23
The Lord is my shepherd; I have what I
need. He lets me lie down in green pastures;
he leads me beside quiet waters. He renews
my life; he leads me along the right paths
for his name's sake. Even when I go through
the darkest valley, I fear no danger, for you
are with me; your rod and your staff—
they comfort me. You prepare a table before
me in the presence of my enemies;
you anoint my head with oil; my cup
overflows. Only goodness and faithful
love will pursue me all the days of my life,
and I will dwell in the house of
the Lord as long as I live.

1 PETER 1:3-7

Blessed be the God and Father of our Lord Jesus Christ. Because of his great mercy he has given us new birth into a living hope through the resurrection of Jesus Christ from the dead and into an inheritance that is imperishable, undefiled, and unfading, kept in heaven for you. You are being guarded by God's power through faith for a salvation that is ready to be revealed in the last time. You rejoice in this, even though now for a short time, if necessary, you suffer grief in various trials so that the proven character of your faith—more valuable than gold which, though perishable, is refined by fire—may result in praise, glory, and honor at the revelation of Jesus Christ.

> *God is our refuge and strength,*
> A HELPER WHO IS ALWAYS
> FOUND IN TIMES OF TROUBLE

BODY PAIN OR SICKNESS

Grief is exhausting. If you have recently endured a loss, your body is experiencing significant stress. Grief takes a toll on our physical bodies, often in the form of tears, headaches, backaches, and sleepless nights. It affects every area of our lives. As a result, it is not uncommon to become physically sick in the midst of our grief.

While this is normal, try to remember to take care of your body. Create rhythms to:

- *Take daily vitamins. Set an alarm on your phone, or put your vitamins in a place where you will see them every morning.*
- *Eat healthy meals, and drink enough water. In grief, you may lose your appetite and not desire food. As much as possible, try to take care of your body so that you can continue to mourn properly without also enduring physical illness.*
- *Get outside in nature, and let the sun shine on your face. Go for a walk, and get regular exercise.*

In Scripture, the psalms are peppered with similar physical struggles. In Psalm 38:3, 6-8, David cries out to the Lord saying, "There is no soundness in my body… no health in my bones… all day long I go around in mourning. For my insides are full of burning pain, and there is no soundness in my body. I am faint and severely crushed; I groan because of the anguish of my heart." His strength had left him, and loved ones had abandoned him. He cries out to the Lord in his pain and reminds himself of the One who brings hope and healing.

If you are struggling with physical pain or sickness, cry out to the Lord. Use the words of David in Psalm 38 to express your pain and grief. Journal your anguish, grief, and sickness. Remind yourself of the promises and hope of God, and ask Him to sustain you.

A WELLNESS CHECK-LIST

In the midst of a physically stressful time, create regular rhythms to protect your body. This list might include the following action steps:

- ☐ *Talk to God, and read His Word*
- ☐ *Take vitamins*
- ☐ *Go for a walk*
- ☐ *Drink water*
- ☐ *Eat regular, healthy meals*
- ☐ *Call a friend*
- ☐ _____

(write in your own action plan)

- ☐ _____
- ☐ _____
- ☐ _____
- ☐ _____
- ☐ _____
- ☐ _____

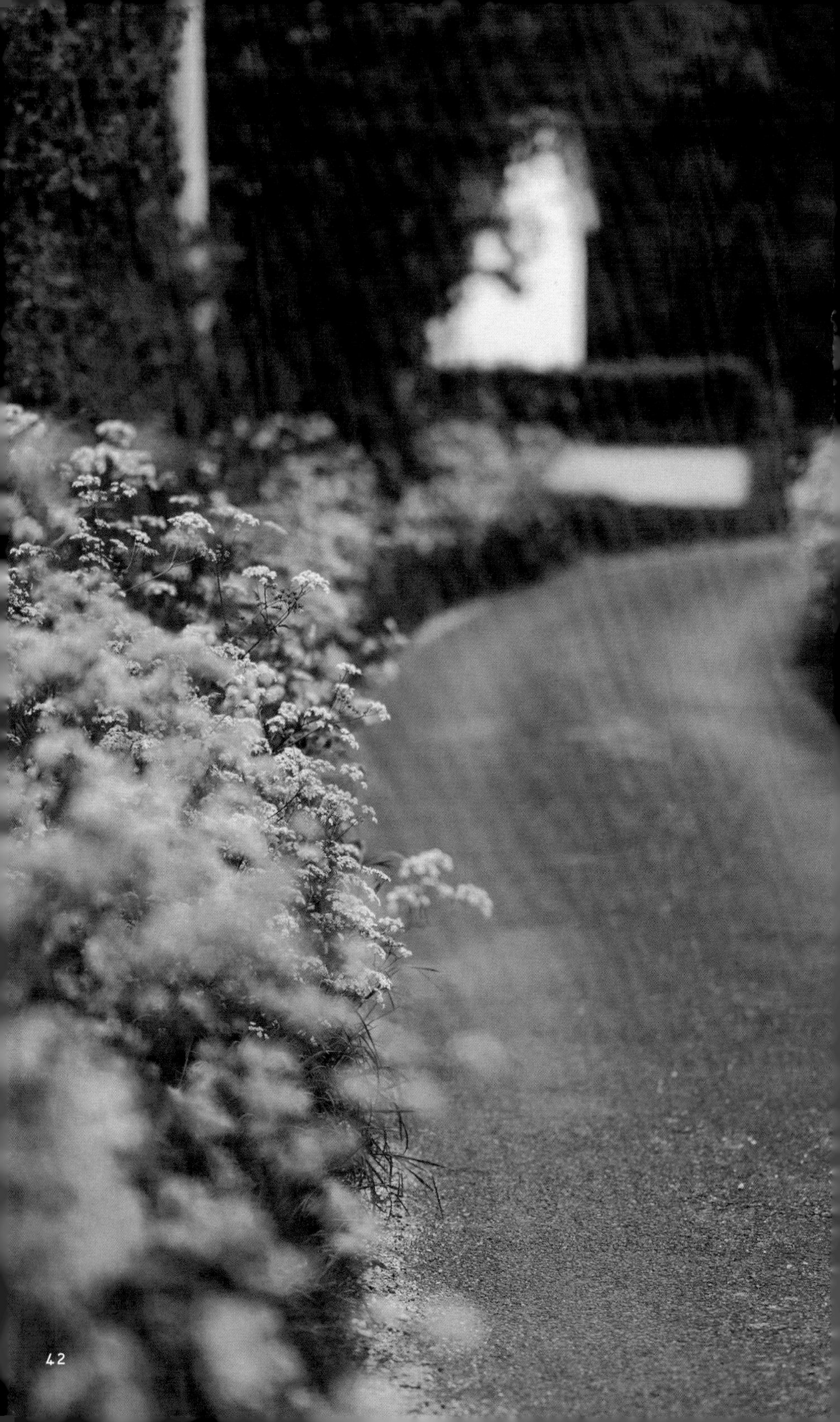

—04—

EMOTIONAL RESPONSES TO GRIEF

Sadness
Bargaining
Loneliness
Guilt, Shame, and Regret
Suicidal Thoughts
Apathy
Anger
Envy
Relief
Anxiety

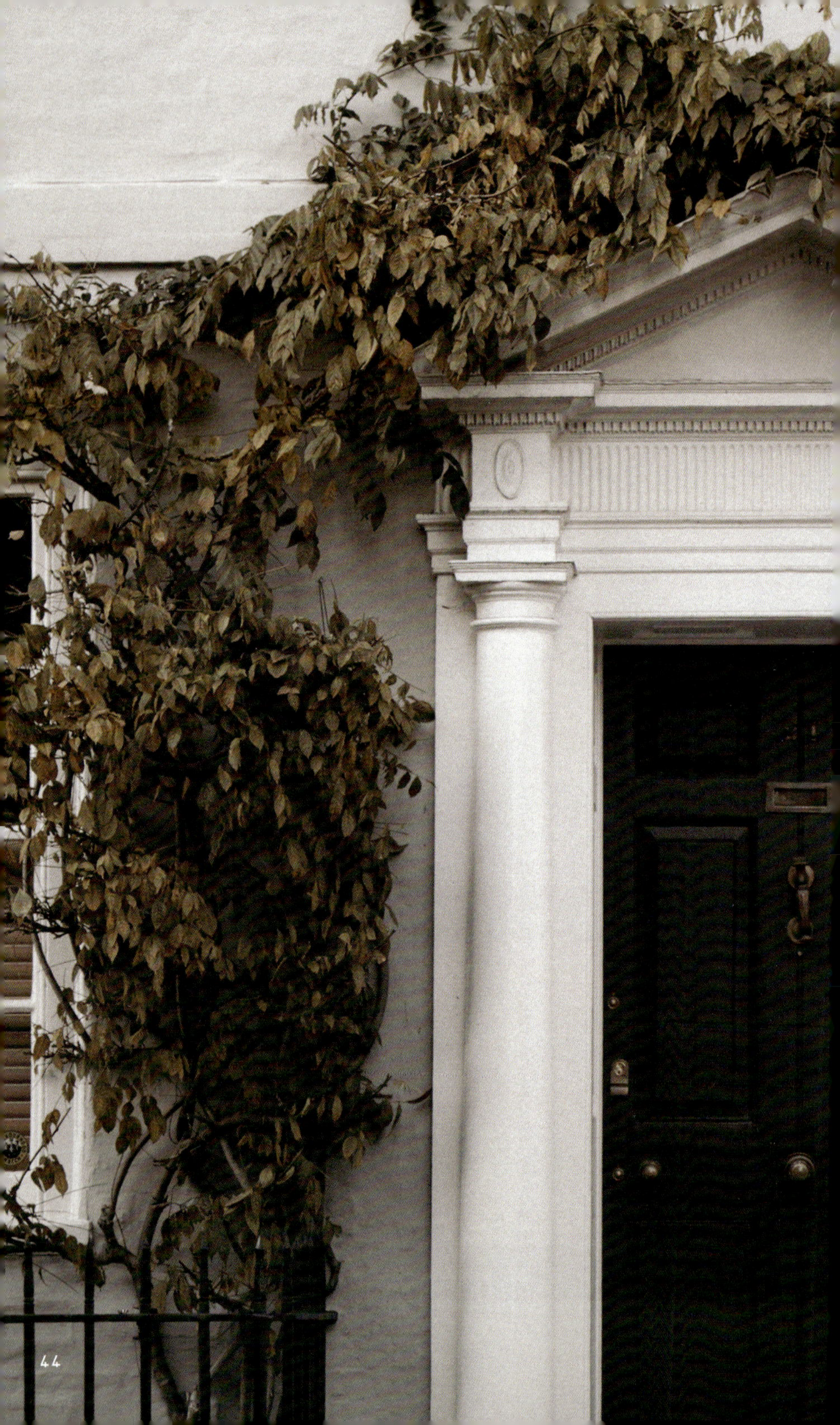

Traditionally, the stages of grief are denial, bargaining, anger, depression, and acceptance. While these are helpful categories, many other emotions may accompany your grief. Perhaps you are picking this book up because you are reeling with envy, anger, or regret in the face of your loss. Or maybe you cannot get out of bed due to depression, loneliness, or despair. Your emotions may ebb and flow, intensifying to unbreathable heights and dropping to numbing lows. You may even experience more than one emotion at the same time. You may experience every emotion expressed in this booklet, or you may experience an entirely different emotion altogether. Each person's grief is unique and can appear differently. Use this section as a template to process your particular grief journey, and discover how the Bible speaks to every one of our emotional experiences.

- *What is your primary expression of grief?*
- *If this emotion could talk, what would it say?*
- *Where do you see God in the midst of this emotion?*

SADNESS

Grief is often described as the dark night of the soul. Sadness follows you like a malnourished, stray cat that clings and nips at your soul until you have nothing left to give. The moment you feel that you can finally escape its famished stare, it tugs you back down into a world of darkness. Your senses feel dulled, and life feels grey. A palpable black cloud follows you, blocking even the memory of happier days.

Sadness amid grief is normal. It is an emotional and honest response to your loss. Even Jesus cried when facing the death of a friend (John 11:35) and was overwhelmed with sadness before enduring the cross (Luke 22:43-44). In our tears and despair, we express how much we loved who or what we lost.

Sometimes we can assume that our sadness is off-putting to God and that we must hide it from Him. As we study the words of Scripture though, we discover that God is not a stoic, asking us to numb our tears or avoid our pain. He is with us in it, and He mourns with us. God is with you in your sadness. He is offering you hope.

Not only this, but Christ intentionally entered into our pain when He came to earth that homely night. He endured the greatest loss, bearing our sins on the cross and paying their penalty with His life. His sympathy for you is great because He knows what it means to suffer. He was rejected by man, and despised. He was weary and full of sorrow. He is not lording Himself over you as a spiteful taskmaster. He is tender and compassionate, and He weeps with you.

Even our sadness can have an eternal purpose. As Paul and his traveling companions traveled, they faced unbearable suffering. They felt like they had received the sentence of death and despaired of life itself because of the trials they faced (2 Corinthians 1:8-9). They were so overwhelmed, beyond their strength, that they did not want to live any longer. Perhaps you know the feeling. But even then, Paul concluded that this happened "so that [they] would not trust in [themselves] but in God who raises the dead." God comforted them in their despair and strengthened their confidence in Him. Our God, who is with us in our sadness, promises to use this loss to strengthen us and refine us in His image.

Even our sadness will one day come to an end. While this weeping may last for the night, joy will come in the morning. In our sorrow, we need more than a happy tune. We need eternal hope (1 Thessalonians 4:13).

A Prayer of Sadness

Lord, I cannot breathe. My sadness is too great for me. The world feels dark, empty, and unbearable. Some days I feel numb. Other days I cannot stop crying. My tears surprise me in the most unexpected times, when I see a butterfly, when I'm cooking pasta, or when I'm driving. I do not know how to face tomorrow, let alone finish today.

Even in my sadness, I know that You are here. You hold me together, and You are my help. You are close. You sympathize with me because You know what it means to suffer. I can cry out to You because I know that You hear me. I know You understand. Lord, please help me. The psalmist said that when his soul was heavy, Your consolation brought joy to his soul. He said that You are close to the brokenhearted, and You bind up my wounds. Please do this, I pray. Heal my hurting heart, and help me to come to You in my sadness. Bring comfort, oh King.

Amen.

Scripture to Read

Psalm 23, Matthew 5:4, Revelation 21:4

BARGAINING

Bargaining is trying to make a deal with God. You pray, hope, and plead for God to save your loved one. You replay the day of the loss and think, *"If only I didn't go to the store that morning"* or *"If only he left the house five minutes later."* You may try making a deal with God, negotiating, "If you heal him, God, I'll ____ (stop smoking, become a missionary, stop sleeping around, etc.)." You make a temporary truce with God, hoping to earn God's favor with a promise of good deeds. Maybe you even pray that God would turn back time and change the circumstances. While this is a normal stage of grief, it is also one we must process through in our hearts.

Bargaining says, "If I am good, maybe God will do good to me." But as Christians, we know that we are not in control, and God does not work this way. God is a just God who will one day reward every good and avenge every wrong, but, for now, we live in the in-between. We live in a fallen world where He allows bad things to happen, trusting that He will one day make things right. He is in control of all things, and He has a much bigger plan than we know.

When we find ourselves bargaining with God in our grief, we can recognize this as an opportunity to cry out to Him for help. Crying out to the Lord acknowledges our lack of control and our need for Him. We can honestly express our pain, fears, regrets, and sorrow, knowing that God is King on His throne. We join the psalmists in their words of lament and cry out to the Lord in our pain. We plead for His protection and beg Him for help. And as we actively surrender our loss to the Lord, we find comfort. We may not understand why this tragedy needed to happen, but we can trust in the sovereignty of God. We find peace, knowing that He is in control, and He is good, even when we do not understand His ways.

Verses on the Sovereignty of God

ROMANS 8:28

We know that all things work together
for the good of those who love God,
who are called according to his purpose.

PROVERBS 16:33

The lot is cast into the lap, but its
every decision is from the Lord.

JOB 42:2

I know that you can do anything
and no plan of yours can be thwarted.

LAMENTATIONS 3:37-39

Who is there who speaks and it happens,
unless the Lord has ordained it? Do not
both adversity and good come from the
mouth of the Most High? Why should any
living person complain, any man,
because of the punishment for his sins?

> "
>
> I KNOW THAT YOU CAN
> DO ANYTHING AND
> *no plan of yours can be thwarted*

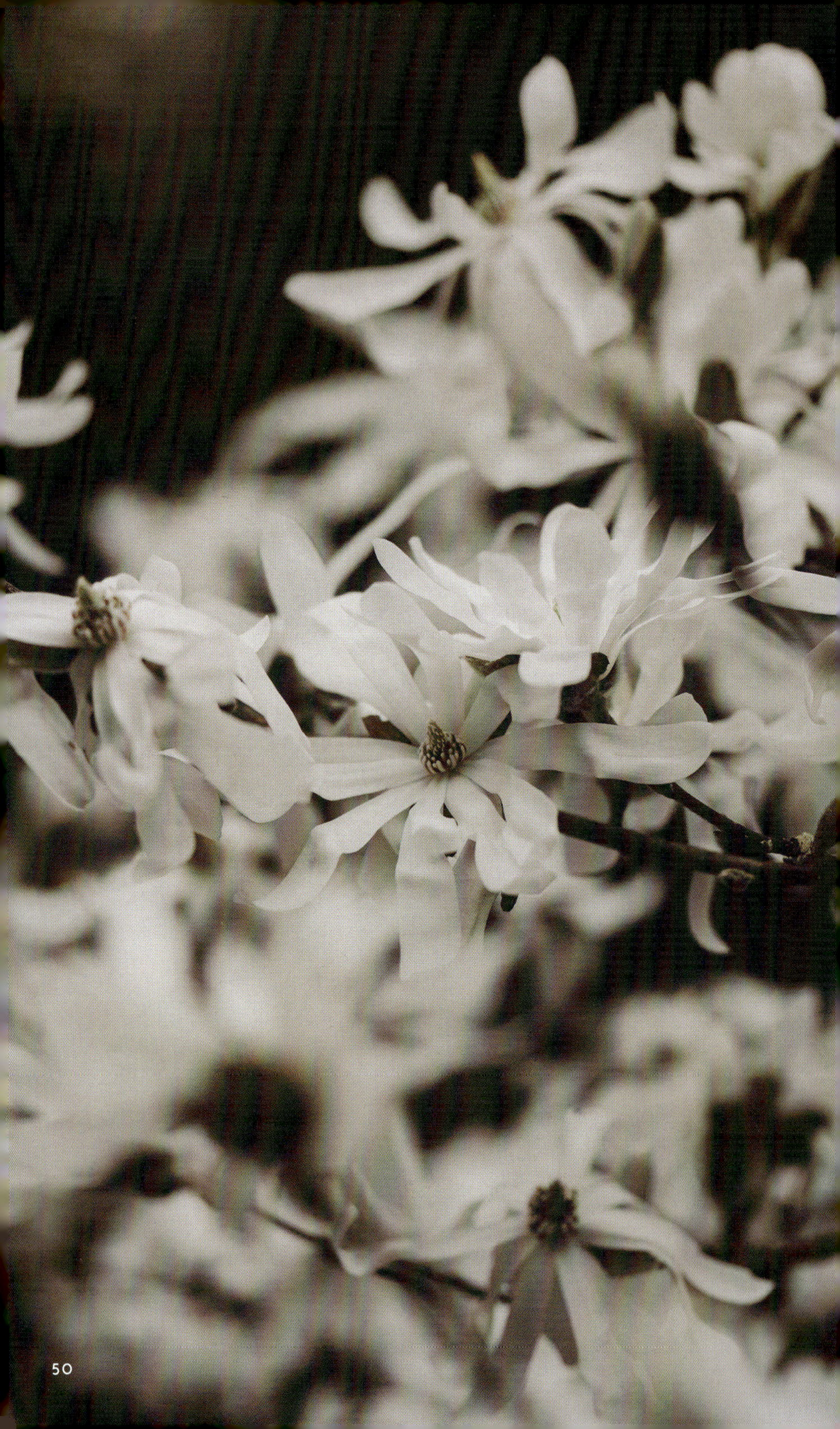

LONELINESS

We can often feel lonely as we process our losses. Maybe you feel abandoned after a difficult breakup. Maybe your ache for a baby in a sea of pregnancy announcements leaves you feeling empty and alone. Or maybe you feel like a third wheel in your friend groups after the loss of your spouse. You feel lonely, even when others are around.

Hear the words of the Lord afresh today when he says, "I am always with you" (Matthew 28:20). Though you cannot see God, He always sees you. He is always listening, always watching, always helping. He never sleeps and is always engaged. He is with you in every season and cares about your concerns.

One beautiful allegory of the Lord's care for us comes from the Chronicles of Narnia by C.S. Lewis. A little boy named Digory went to Aslan to beg for healing for his mother. She had cancer and was going to die. Digory said:

> "But please, please—won't you—cannot you give me something that will cure Mother?" Up till then, he had been looking at the Lion's great feet and the huge claws on them; now, in his despair, he looked up at its face. What he saw surprised him as much as anything in his whole life. For the tawny face was bent down near his own and (wonder of wonders) great shining tears stood in the Lion's eyes. They were such big, bright tears compared with Digory's own that for a moment he felt as if the Lion must really be sorrier about his mother than he was himself. "My son, my son," said Aslan. "I know. Grief is great."

Though grief may make us feel alone, God has not forsaken us. He is with us in our grief, and He understands.

It is also important to continue to pursue community, even in the midst of grief. While it can be tempting to withdraw from friends or family in our mourning, it is especially important to create a network of support. In time, this will also help broaden your perspective and strengthen your faith. As you continue on your grief journey, find ways to serve others around you.

> THOUGH GRIEF MAY MAKE US FEEL ALONE, *God has not forsaken us*

Help for Lonely Days

On lonely days, we must renew our minds with the truth of God's Word. He has given us His presence and the local church to strengthen us.

Look up the following verses. What do they teach you about God's character and presence?

JOHN 14:18

PSALM 147:3

ISAIAH 43:1-3

Help for Lonely Days

Look up the following verses. What do they teach you about God's character and presence?

PSALM 27:10

I TIMOTHY 1:14-17

Make a list of the people God has placed in your life. When you are ready in your stage of grief, make a plan to follow up with them. Some ideas may include giving someone a call, inviting them over, making cookies for someone who is sick, etc.

NAME	ACTION STEP

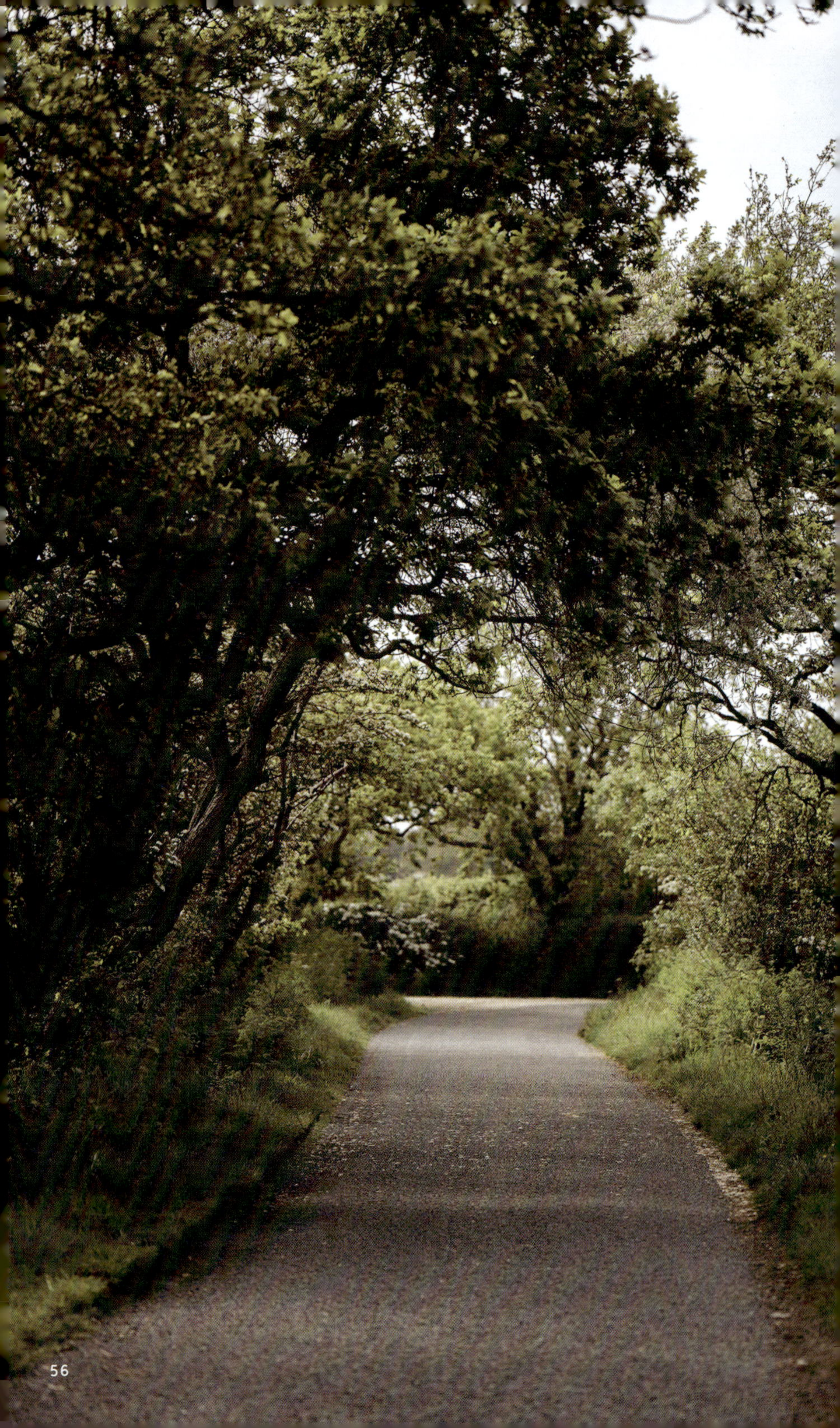

GUILT, SHAME, AND REGRET

Are you struggling with guilt, shame, or regret? Maybe you feel guilty for a wrong committed against the one you have lost. You were driving the car that caused the accident. You may experience survivor guilt, feeling guilty for living when those around you have died. You feel guilty that you can go to your child's graduation, pick out another Christmas tree, and have another meal when others cannot. You may even feel guilty receiving a financial inheritance or insurance benefits from the loss of your loved one. Or maybe you feel shame for that mean word you spoke. You did not know it would be the last time you would speak with your loved one. Maybe you regret not saying "I love you" more or not calling the doctor sooner when you started noticing symptoms of a learning disability in your child. Or maybe you wish you had worked harder at your job, making yourself indispensable so that your boss would never even think about firing you.

Part of the grieving process is the ability to see the past clearly, remembering the good and the bad memories of the one we have lost. In our grief, we have the tendency to meditate on our failures and the other's successes. We dwell on all the bad things we have done and remember the best characteristics of the one we have lost. Wearing "graduation goggles," we think that everything looked beautiful in our past. The job we lost was perfect. Our loved ones never yelled. We were always the ones who made the mistakes. In time, we must try to recall an accurate picture of our loved ones.

If you have active regrets, write them down, and ask the Lord to take them from your heart and mind. Maybe you have done something wrong. Everyone has. These moments are in the past and cannot be changed. While it may be difficult to name your regrets, the Lord is able and willing to forgive all of your sins and cover your shame. Bring your guilt and shame to the Lord, and ask for His forgiveness. He has provided a way for us to be healed through His Son. You can be free from your guilt, shame, and regret by trusting in God's perfect forgiveness.

Healing from Guilt, Shame, and Regret

Make a list of your regrets, guilty feelings, or shameful moments. Then prayerfully bring them to the Lord.

Prayerfully bring them to the Lord with a prayer, such as:

Lord, I'm feeling guilty and ashamed. I wish I had acted differently, spoke differently, lived differently. Would You please forgive me of my sins? Would You take these regrets from my mind? I know I cannot reconcile these feelings with the one I lost. Would You help me find peace, knowing that You provide whole and lasting forgiveness for me? Jesus paid for my sins once and for all on the cross. Through His perfect sacrifice, He has taken away my shame and given me His perfection. Help me remember this truth and live in the freedom that You offer me today.

Amen.

> YOU CAN BE FREE FROM YOUR GUILT, SHAME, AND REGRET BY *trusting in God's perfect forgiveness*

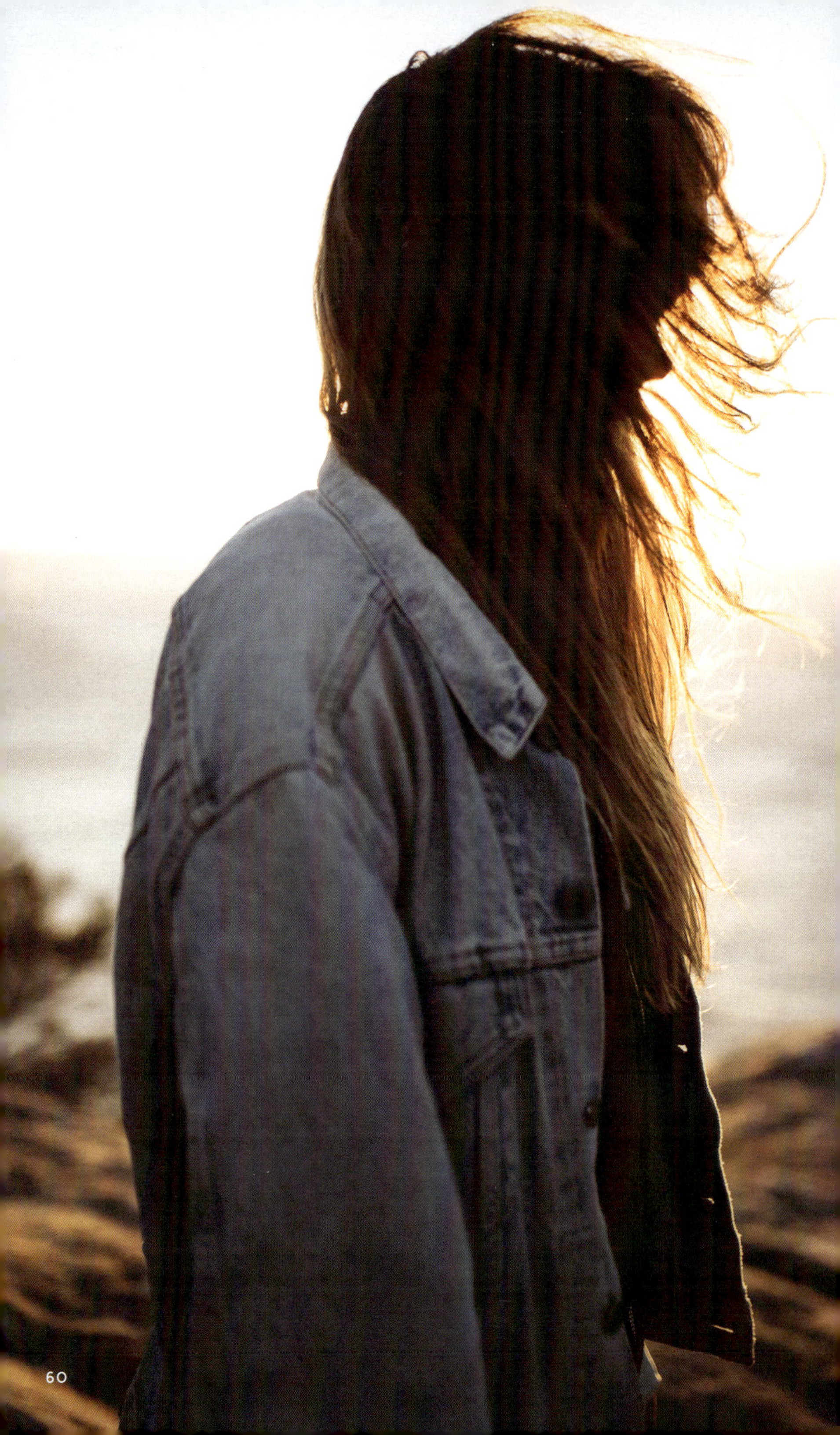

SUICIDAL THOUGHTS

At times, despair may lead you to a deep darkness of the soul. You cannot imagine a time when your pain will end. Life feels unbearable, and grief often brings death naturally to mind. Death may even seem like a sweet escape or a welcomed opportunity to be with your loved one again. You may desire to end your life. If you are experiencing suicidal thoughts, talk to someone right away. While it is normal to experience these thoughts, in periods of grief, it is important that you share this with your pastor or a trusted biblical counselor. Until then, do not consume any alcohol, drugs, or anything that lowers your inhibitions to harm yourself. Even though you may not be able to see it now, there is still hope. God is with you in your confusion, grief, and hopelessness. He longs to give you hope, and suicide is not the answer.

If a loved one expresses to you that they have been thinking about hurting themselves, take them seriously. Pray for them, ask good questions, and listen to their story. Sometimes, our friends may not have a suicidal plan, but they are feeling dark and hopeless. Help your friend understand the pain they are feeling, and share the hope available to them in Christ. At other times, your friend may be actively considering suicide and formulating a plan to hurt themselves. Ask him or her if they have made a plan about how they would hurt themselves. Ask them who else you can call at that moment, including their pastor, a counselor, or a mental health facility. Enlarge the group of people who can help. Pray for the Lord's help, and if you are concerned that your friend is imminently suicidal, do not let them leave your presence. In these crisis moments, take comfort that God is with you and will guide you.

For immediate help, contact the Suicide Helpline: 1-800-273-8255.

Write Your Own Prayer of Lament

A prayer of lament is a way to process grief in a way that expresses our pain and anguish to the Lord in the midst of tragedies, disasters, and disappointments. Prayers of lament do not sugarcoat our emotions or ignore our pain. Instead, they bring them all to the Lord with wrestling and faith.

Our laments reconcile what we know to be true with the pain of our reality. What an act of faith to cry out to the Lord, acknowledging Christ's sovereignty, power, and love while, at the same time, fighting to see those things in your circumstances. Even still, we come to Him. In our pain and suffering, we bring the Lord our concerns and ask for Him to move. As we do so, our faith is renewed.

The Bible is rich with prayers of lament in books of the Bible such as Habakkuk, Job, and Psalms. Read Psalm 6, 10, and 22, and write your own prayer of lament. Using Psalm 22 as a template, write a prayer that includes details from your own life. In your suffering, appeal to God for help because of His goodness and love.

My Prayer of Lament

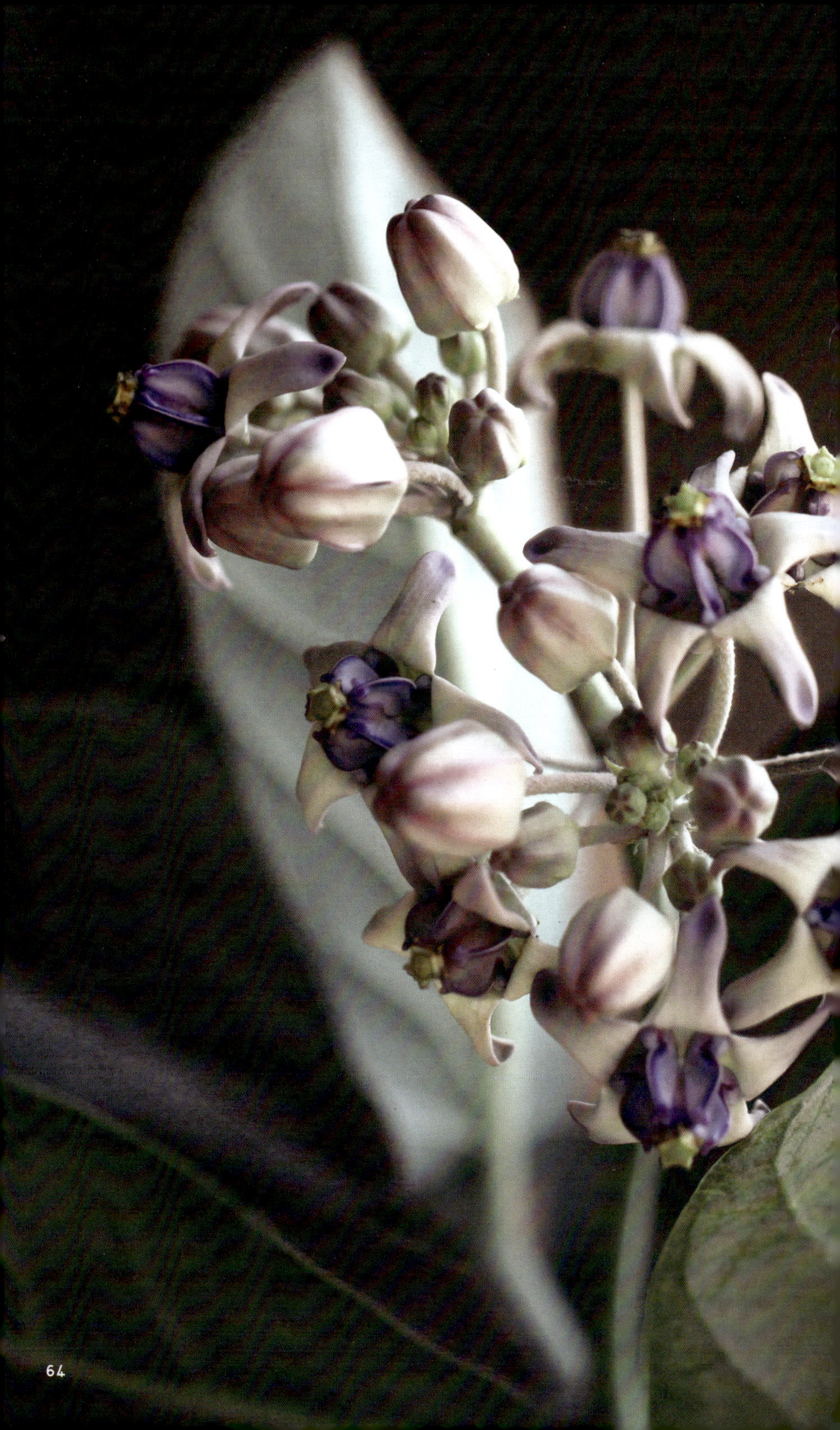

APATHY

Are you having trouble enjoying activities you once enjoyed? After a loss, our priorities often change. Hobbies we once loved seem to lose their allure. Your old life feels like a pair of old shoes. It does not seem to fit anymore. The past seems a distant memory. Nothing seems to matter anymore, and feeling anything seems like an impossible task. Numbness and apathy are often disorienting. At the same time, they are normal emotional responses to shock (see page 21).

While it can be easier to avoid all feelings instead of facing our pain, the Lord, in His kindness, gives us the strength to do so. This can be understanding our external reality and our internal suffering. When we face these realities head-on, we can discover the hope available to us through the gospel. Although changing priorities can be baffling, they can also be a gift. Maybe you realize that you were putting too much value in your appearance, your material belongings, or your work. While these are not inherently bad, your priorities have changed. You realize that everything will fade away, including your physical body and that shiny new car. As an overcorrection, you may not value anything, but in time, you have the opportunity to recenter your world with a foundation of godly priorities.

In Christ, we also have the freedom to express all of our emotions to the Lord in prayer. We can share our apathy, our numbness, and our confusion. We see this in David, who prayed, "How long, O Lord? Will you forget me forever?" (Psalm 13:1) and "You have put me in the lowest part of the Pit, in the darkest places, in the depths" (Psalm 88:6). Even Jesus cried prayers of candor, "My God, my God, why have you abandoned me?" (Matthew 27:46). While you are experiencing apathy, continue to communicate with the Lord about all things. Because Christ died on the cross for us, we can approach the future with confidence, knowing that our greatest problem has been dealt with. If He gave us His own Son, how will He not also help us in this season? Even though you may be feeling numb, the Lord's loving empathy, care, and love toward you never grows cold. He is fully engaged with you in every way, deeply grieving your loss and sustaining you with His never-ending affection.

> **WHILE YOU ARE EXPERIENCING APATHY, CONTINUE TO COMMUNICATE WITH THE LORD** *about all things.*

Suggested Activities in a Season of Apathy

- *Have grace with yourself. This too shall pass, and in time you will experience a wide array of emotions, from anger to joy.*
- *Consider your history of loss. Have you ever experienced something like this before? How did you respond? What has helped you in difficult seasons in the past?*
- *Pray, and express your thoughts, concerns, and numbness to the Lord.*
- *Write a letter to God or a loved one about your loss. Sometimes writing our thoughts can encourage internal candor that we are not willing to admit otherwise.*
- *Find intentional ways to engage with the world. Consider going on a walk and looking around to notice the details of God's creation.*
- *Take care of your body by engaging in healthy habits.*
- *Find ways to invest in others in your local church.*
- *Ask how you can be praying for others.*

ANGER

Anger is a natural response to pain. In our suffering, we rage against the brokenness of this world. We look for a reason for our loss and for someone to blame. We feel a deep, blinding fury, a red hot passion that consumes everything in its path. Our emotion screams, "Injustice! This should not have happened!"

In seasons of grieving, we can aim our feelings of anger toward God, ourselves, or others.

Spend a moment to evaluate the direction of your anger. Are you angry at God because He allowed this painful circumstance to occur? Are you mad at others because of insensitive or unhelpful words? Are you mad at the doctor who could not save your loved one, or even possibly, at the person who died? Or are you angry with yourself because you could not stop this loss from happening? As Christians, we must actively reorient our anger by meditating on the truths found in Scripture. When we do so, we remember:

1. *God is in control.* He has not left His throne, and this did not catch Him by surprise. He did not stop being good, even at the moment of our deepest pain. He is still present, still powerful, and still good. Though we cannot always see it, God will mysteriously work through every broken reality for His glory and our good (Romans 8:28). Even when people fail us, God does not ignore a single tear. He is present, and He cares.

2. *There is brokenness in the world.* Our anger and pain reflect the brokenness of this world and our need for a Savior.

3. *God will make everything right.* One day, God will right every wrong. He will lead us to His eternal kingdom where there is no more death, crying, pain, or mourning (Revelation 21:4). He will display His perfect justice and vengeance (Hebrews 10:30). We wait with eager expectation for His perfect wisdom to be displayed.

> EVEN WHEN PEOPLE FAIL US,
> GOD DOES NOT IGNORE
> *a single tear*

Anger Analysis

Spend time evaluating your anger:

TO WHOM ARE YOU DIRECTING YOUR ANGER?

___

WHY ARE YOU ANGRY?

___

WHAT DOES SCRIPTURE SAY ABOUT ANGER?
Read Leviticus 19:16-18, Hebrews 10:30, and Ephesians 4:26-27

Write a prayer to the Lord expressing your anger, repenting of any sinful anger, and asking for His help.

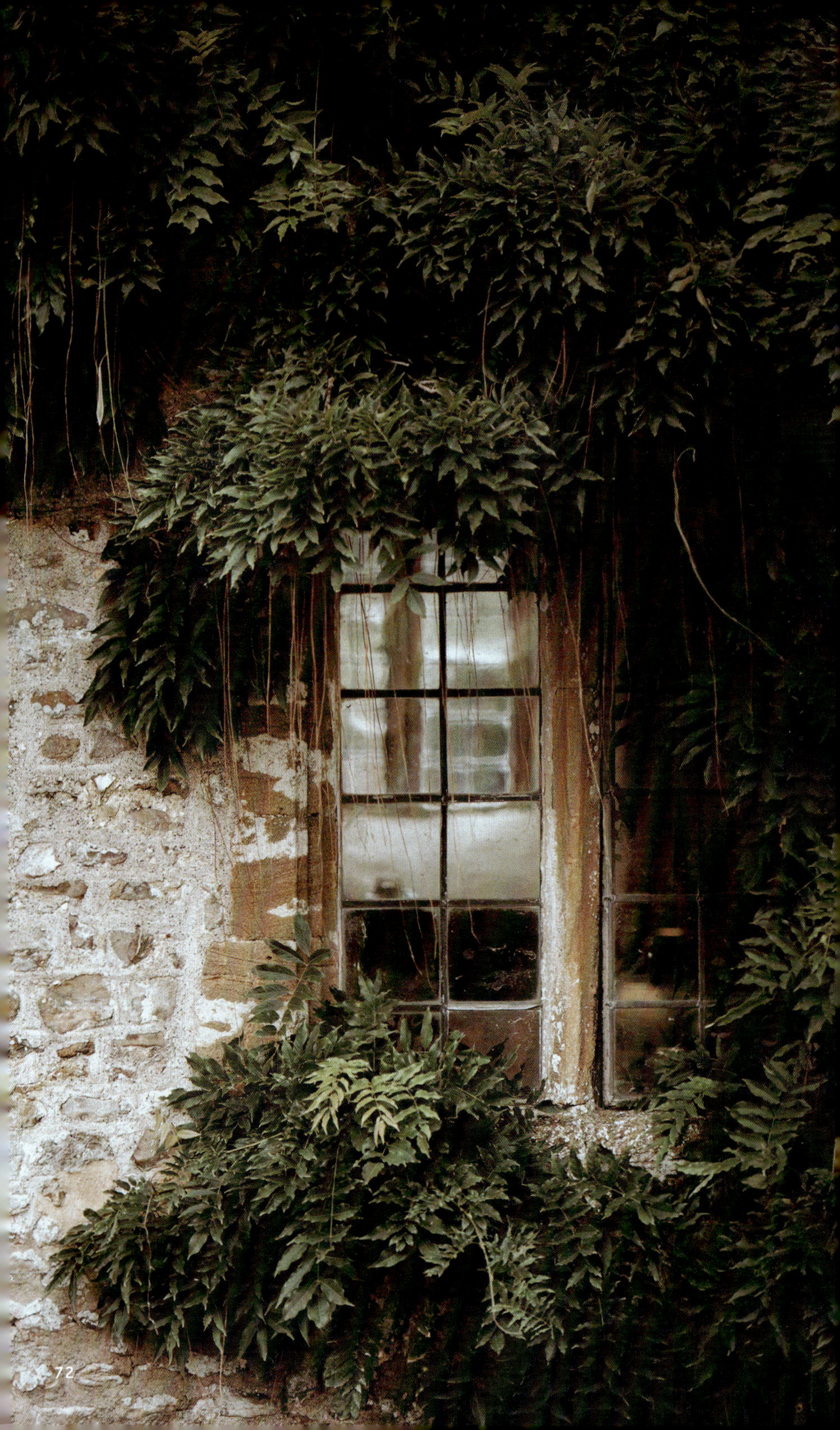

ENVY

In grief, our whole world has changed. We have lost something, or someone, of great significance. Time seems to have stopped. Happiness evades us. But for those around us, the world has continued at full speed. Our friends keep getting married, having babies, and getting promotions. They celebrate Christmas like usual, without a raw, gnawing pain consuming their insides. You may begin to envy their lives, happiness, relational status, or ignorance of the pain of this world. You envy those who can make new memories with their loved ones. You envy those who got to say goodbye. You envy those with happier days or happier lives.

The Bible is not quiet on the topic of envy. Envy was expressed from the beginning with the murder of Abel (Genesis 4:3-8) and in Esau's pursuit of Jacob (Genesis 27:41). It was also expressed in childbearing when Rachel could not bear children, but her sister could (Genesis 30:1). While envy is focused on disappointment and dissatisfaction, the opposite of envy is contentment.

In our struggle for contentment, we must preach the gospel to ourselves as David and other writers did in the psalms. In Psalm 73, the psalmist struggled with jealousy. He evaluated the blessings of the wicked and envied their lives of happiness and ease. They did not struggle or grieve. They were not sick or tired. Instead, they seemed cheery and prosperous. It was not until the psalmist fixed his eyes on eternity that he remembered their end: God was going to make everything right in the end, and the wicked would receive their just punishment. The psalmist preached the truths of Scripture to himself and ended with a redirected focus on the Lord, "Who do I have in heaven but you? And I desire nothing on earth but you. My flesh and my heart may fail, but God is the strength of my heart, my portion forever" (Psalm 73:25-26).

Although contentment may feel impossible in a season of grief, we can find peace in the constant presence of the Lord. He controls our days, and He is trustworthy. In faith, we long for His justice and rest in His love. We renew our minds in the promises of Scripture and bring all of our emotions before the Lord in prayer.

> "
> ALTHOUGH CONTENTMENT MAY FEEL IMPOSSIBLE IN A SEASON OF GRIEF, WE CAN FIND PEACE IN THE *constant presence of the Lord*

Gratitude List

Grief is an expression of love. We have lost something or someone whom we loved. Memories of happier days are gone, and the world tastes sour. In our grief, emotions such as anger and sadness can often cover over happier memories. As an act of remembrance today, write a list of thankfulness and gratitude. If you are in a fresh season of grief, be patient with yourself. Your pain may be too raw for this exercise. If necessary, come back to this application at a later time.

Write a list of gratitude for the one you have lost. Examples may include specific memories, dreams answered, seasons of joy, specific personality traits, etc.

Gratitude List

Write a list of gratitude for the current blessings in your life. If life feels especially dark, this may include a simple list such as air to breathe, food to eat, or clothes to wear. No item, blessing, or person is too small to bring before the Lord in thanksgiving.

What attributes of God have helped you in your season of grief? Direct your thanksgiving to the Lord for His faithfulness, kindness, gentleness, etc.

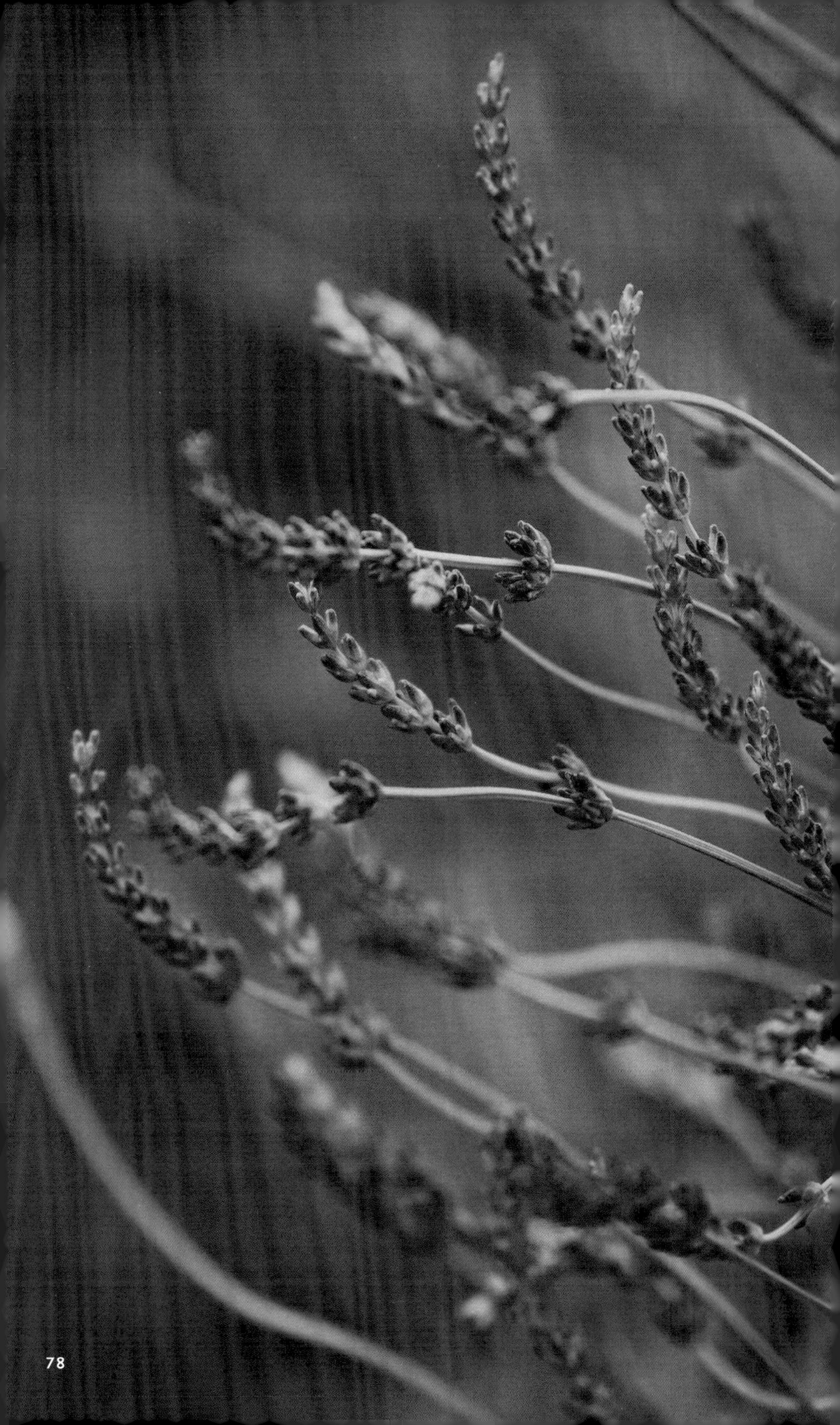

RELIEF

Maybe as you have been reading, you have felt a sense of shame growing in your heart. You have not identified with feelings of guilt or anger. Instead, you feel relieved. Maybe you lost an abusive family member who hurt you deeply during their lifetime. Or perhaps your loved one was in debilitating pain for many years. Although you miss them, you are also relieved that they are no longer suffering. You are relieved that the doctor's appointments and the need for constant medical attention have ended. It feels like a burden has been lifted. You may wonder if you are a bad person for feeling this way.

While many people do not talk about the feeling of relief, it is also a normal emotion. When difficult relationships end or when a loved one is no longer in pain, there can be a sense of reassurance and peace. Relief does not necessarily mean that you wanted this loss. It does not mean that you hated the person who died or that you wanted them to pass away. It can simply be a sign that a difficult season has ended.

The first step to processing your relief is to admit it to yourself and the Lord. Talk to the Lord about how you are feeling. Write in a prayer journal if helpful. Examine your heart for any bitterness or hidden resentment, and if present, confess them to the Lord. Share your emotions with a trusted friend who would understand. Then, find peace in the sovereignty of God, who is in control of all things. If helpful, talk to a counselor or trusted friend in depth to continue your grieving process.

A Prayer of Surrender and Relief

Lord, You are in control of all things. I come to You today feeling relief that a difficult season has ended. I feel guilty for feeling that way, but I'm also breathing easier knowing that _____ has ended. Father, You are my King and my Lord. You are the one who holds the world together. You knew that this would happen, and You know what will happen tomorrow. I know that I cannot control my world as much as I wish I could at times.

As I process this loss, help me press into You. Let me not become selfish or self-reliant but follow You in every season of life. Use this next season of my life to bring You glory. Use my time, my treasures, my freedom, and my pain to make Your name famous. Help me grieve well and accept this loss with grace and faith.

Amen.

ANXIETY

Will I forget them? What happens tomorrow? Who's next? How am I going to make it? This is too much for me! Anxiety can feel like a scratchy rope wrapped tightly around your ankles. You try to swim, but it abruptly yanks you down under the water. Gasping for air, you flail about, desperate for air. The moment you think you have made it, that the coast is clear, it unexpectedly pulls you down again. It leaves you breathless, feeling like you are drowning.

Anxiety is a normal response after trauma. In our grief, we are harshly confronted by our lack of control in life. The future feels unstable and unpredictable. You feel unsure of what tomorrow will bring. You may feel jittery at every phone call and knock on the door after receiving your bad news. You may fear the silence, not knowing when the next wave of grief or tragedy will come. You may feel disoriented, freshly aware of your mortality. You might be afraid of getting close to someone again because you are afraid they'll leave. Or maybe your desires become inextricably mixed. You simultaneously long for, and are deathly afraid of, getting pregnant again after your miscarriages. Fear and longing fuse intimately together.

In our anxiety, we bring tomorrow's problems into today. Our minds run wild with all of the "what-ifs" of tomorrow — these scenarios drain our energy for today. The psalmist of Psalm 46 understood this experience well. Facing real sorrow and uncertainty, he was afraid. Still, he slowed and calmed his heart in order to focus on what was true. He said, "God is our refuge and strength, a helper who is always found in times of trouble. Therefore we will not be afraid, though the earth trembles and the mountains topple into the depths of the seas" (Psalm 46:1-2). Although scary, life-altering earthquakes and tsunamis are mentioned, the psalmist reminds his heart that he does not need to fear because God is with him.

The antidote for anxiety is to meditate on what is true. God's character and protection do not change, no matter how scary the present may seem. In your battle against anxiety, search the Scriptures to discover what the Bible says about fear, uncertainty, and death. Find a biblical counselor or trusted friend with whom you can discuss your fears. Write, sing, paint, or journal your experience with grief. Express all your thoughts, prayers, and fears to the Lord, and meditate on the rock-solid promises of Scripture.

Combating Anxiety Using Psalm 46

Read Psalm 46, and mark it using the following key:

- *Underline the promises of God.*
- *Circle the scary circumstances mentioned in the psalm.*
- *Star the emotions expressed by the psalmists.*
- *Highlight the character and presence of God.*
- *Make a box around verses 10-11. What do these verses teach us about the cure for anxiety?*

Psalm 46

1 God is our refuge and strength,
a helper who is always found
in times of trouble.
2 Therefore we will not be afraid,
though the earth trembles
and the mountains topple
into the depths of the seas,
3 though its water roars and foams
and the mountains quake with its turmoil.
4 There is a river—
its streams delight the city of God,
the holy dwelling place of the Most High.
5 God is within her; she will not be toppled.
God will help her when the morning dawns.
6 Nations rage, kingdoms topple;
the earth melts when he lifts his voice.
7 The Lord of Armies is with us;
the God of Jacob is our stronghold.
8 Come, see the works of the Lord,
who brings devastation on the earth.
9 He makes wars cease throughout the earth.
He shatters bows and cuts spears to pieces;
he sets wagons ablaze.
10 "Stop your fighting, and know that I am God,
exalted among the nations, exalted on the earth."
11 The Lord of Armies is with us;
the God of Jacob is our stronghold.

What do you learn from the psalmist's encounter with scary realities? How can you apply this to your own life?

Bonus: Choose a section of this psalm to memorize.

> "
> **THE LORD OF ARMIES IS WITH US;
> THE GOD OF JACOB IS**
> *our stronghold*

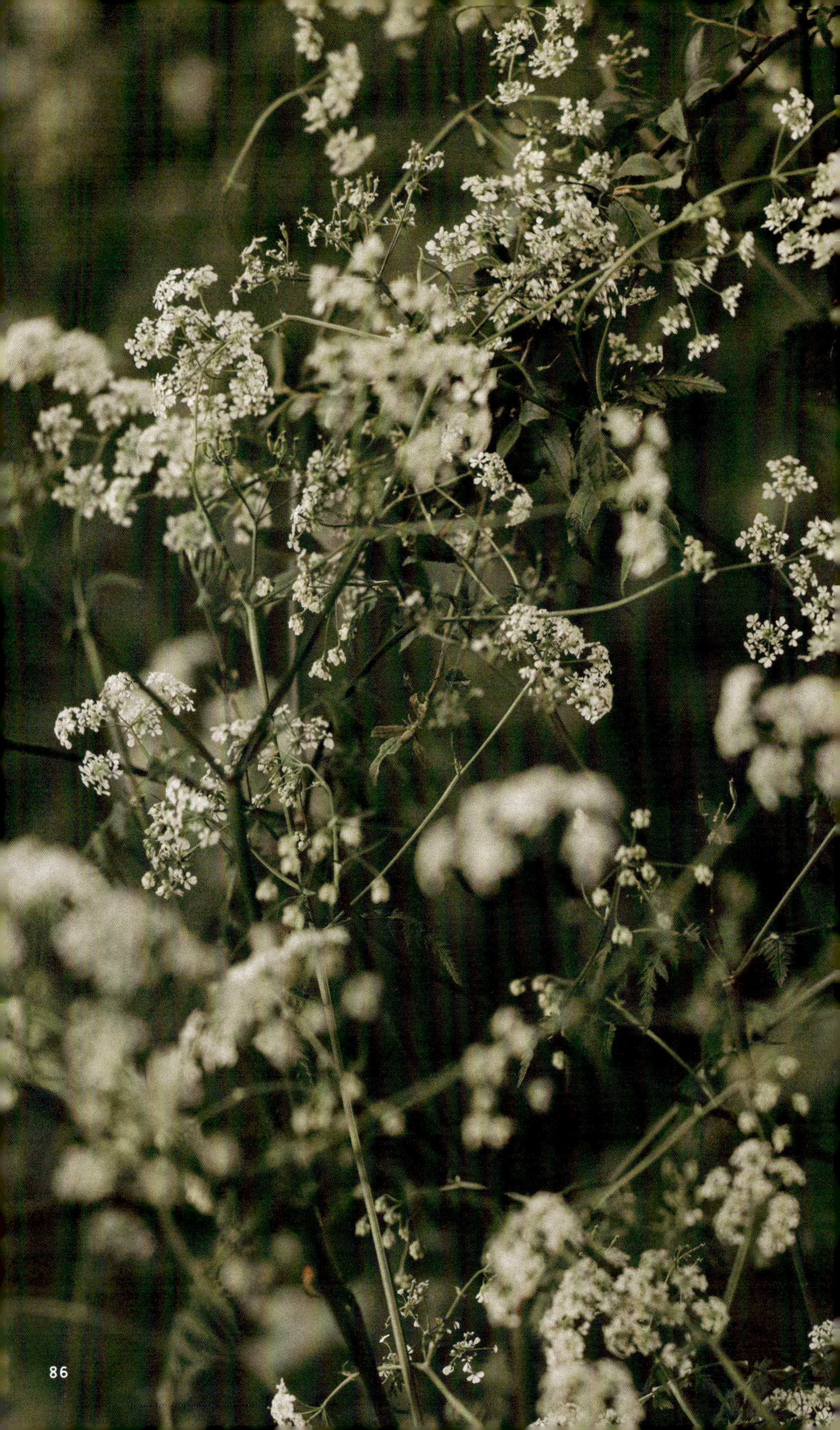

05

SPIRITUAL RESPONSES TO GRIEF

Anger at God
Despair at Living
When God Feels Distant
Purposelessness in Life
Doubt in the Lord's Goodness
Hope in the Lord

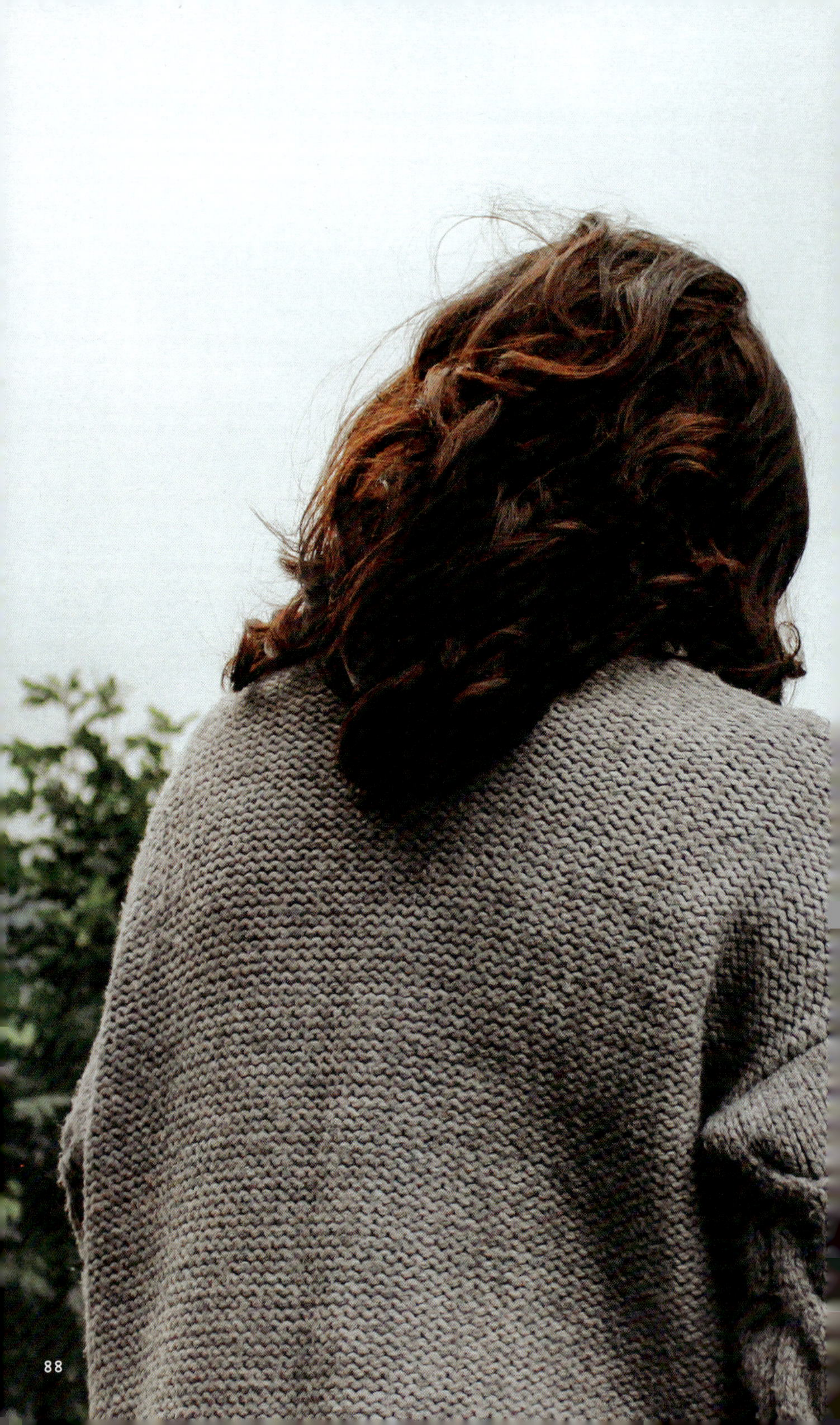

ANGER AT GOD

As Christians, we believe that God is powerful. He holds the whole world in His hands, and He controls all things. He gives us each breath, and every blessing comes from Him. Ironically, these very beliefs can lead us to be angry with God when tragedies strike. We know that because God is all-powerful, He could have prevented our loss from happening. So where is He? Why did He allow these bad things to happen? Our sovereign God has hurt us, and we are mad at Him because of it.

Throughout the Bible, many men have expressed this thought. They were angry when the Lord acted against their desires. In the book of Genesis, Cain was mad that God did not accept his sacrifice, and he murdered his brother in response (Genesis 4:1-16). In the book of Jonah, the prophet was angry with the Lord because He showed mercy on his enemies (Jonah 4:1-4). Even David, a man after God's own heart, was angry at God after He killed Uzzah for touching the ark (2 Samuel 6:1-8).

Although anger is a natural human emotion, we can choose to engage in anger in sinful or non-sinful ways. When we are angry at God, we perceive that He has done something wrong. We wish He would have made other choices. Perhaps we wish He would have saved our loved ones or preserved our health. We replace our trust and joy in Him with anger. But while we know that this kind of anger lacks faith in the goodness of God, we can often feel powerless to combat it. So what are we to do? When we are angry at God, should we shamefully hide our sinful emotions until they go away? By no means. Instead, we bring all our complaints, moanings, and cries to the Lord precisely because we believe that He is in control and He is good.

The Old Testament hero, Job, is a great example of this. When Job lost his children, livestock, and health due to the Lord allowing these tragedies, his first response was to worship. He trusted God despite his overwhelming pain. As time progressed and he processed his losses, Job continued to mourn before the Lord in the form of lament. He brought all of his protests to God. He knew he was innocent and did not deserve the tragedy that was upon him. He raged at the brokenness of the world and cursed the day he was born. He lamented that God would pursue him, seemingly intent to squish him like a bug. He brought His emotions before the Lord, expressing his raw and honest pain to God. He wrestled before God and ultimately submitted to His powerful and sovereign plan.

God can handle our questions. He may not respond to them on this side of eternity, but He does promise us this: He will be with us in our pain. Though we may not understand the "why" behind our sorrow, we can still worship God in our grief and come before Him in lament. As we lament, we go to the Lord in our anger and engage with Him in faith. We come to Him in our pain and plead for His help and guidance. We wrestle with the brokenness of this world in light of eternity. We trust that God is in control and He is good, and we remember that one day, God will make all things right. He will judge the world and wipe every tear. He will take vengeance on the wicked. Until then, we long for His justice as we pour out our hearts to Him.

For more on lament, see pages 62-63 for the lament exercise, or read the book of Habakkuk, Lamentations, and Psalm 88.

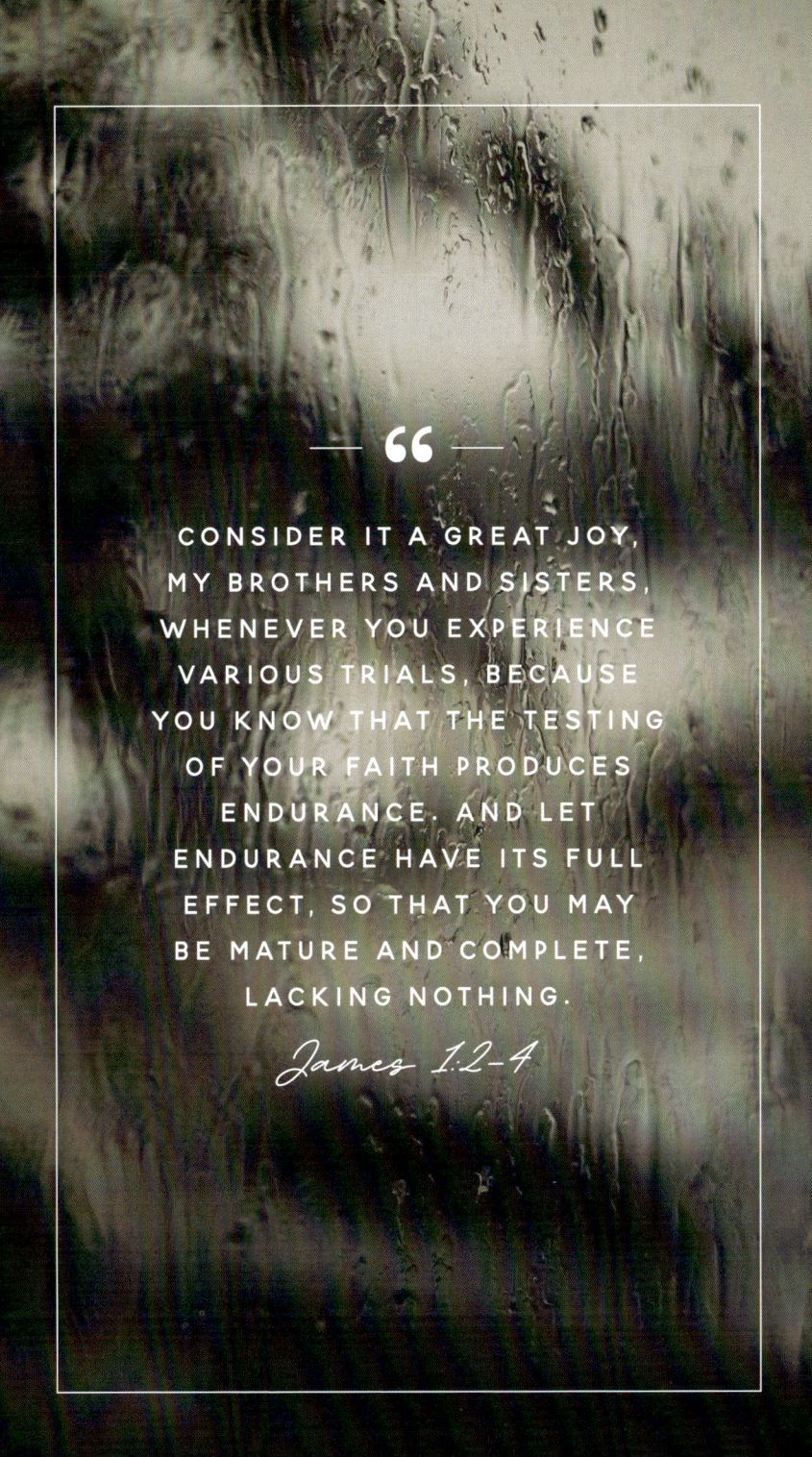

> "Consider it a great joy, my brothers and sisters, whenever you experience various trials, because you know that the testing of your faith produces endurance. And let endurance have its full effect, so that you may be mature and complete, lacking nothing.
>
> *James 1:2-4*

DESPAIR AT LIVING

You have tried praying. You have tried reading the Bible. You have tried talking to your pastor, but nothing makes sense. No one seems to understand. Your prayers feel like they are bouncing off the ceiling, and God feels like He is a million miles away. It feels like the foundation you were standing on has been swept away, and no hope remains. You despair at life itself.

In seasons of grief, we despair because we know that life was not meant to be this way. As we grapple with our losses, we feel sad, hopeless, and are full of misery. We just want our pain to end. The story of Elijah expresses this thought. Elijah was a prophet in the Old Testament who spoke the word of God to the people. He experienced extraordinary displays of God's power, including fire coming down from heaven and the defeat of the prophets of Baal (1 Kings 18:20-40). Yet, when the evil Queen Jezebel heard about these victories, she was furious and demanded that Elijah be killed. Elijah, hearing about this threat, was afraid and ran for his life. He traveled for a day into the wilderness, and lying under a broom tree, asked God that he could die. He said, "I have had enough! Lord, take my life for I'm no better than my fathers" (1 King 19:4). Elijah, who had just seen the Lord's power miraculously displayed, was so tired and discouraged that he wanted the Lord to take his life.

Notice how God responded to Elijah's despair. He did not tell him to "cheer up" or "have more faith." He did not abandon him for a prophet who would have been better equipped, and He did not tell Elijah how disappointed He was in him. Instead, God sent an angel to touch Elijah, saying, "Get up and eat, or the journey will be too much for you" (1 Kings 19:7). The angel touched him, fed him, and took care of his needs. In the next few verses, the Lord continues to remind Elijah of His power and presence (1 Kings 19:13-19) and provides a companion for his journey (1 Kings 19:19-21). The Lord did not condemn Elijah in his despair but cared for him.

In the same way, God does not withdraw from us in our pain or despair. He does not cringe at our tears or find our weakness disgusting. He runs toward us as our Healer to save us and bind up our wounds (Psalm 147:3). He sends people to care for us and equips the local church to help us in our weakness. While our faith may feel shaky, we can press into God's Word to find a lasting hope—a hope that is not conditional on health, money, or relational stability but the unchanging goodness of God.

> THEREFORE WE DO NOT GIVE UP. EVEN THOUGH OUR OUTER PERSON IS BEING DESTROYED, OUR INNER PERSON IS BEING RENEWED DAY BY DAY. FOR OUR MOMENTARY LIGHT AFFLICTION IS PRODUCING FOR US AN ABSOLUTELY INCOMPARABLE ETERNAL WEIGHT OF GLORY. SO WE DO NOT FOCUS ON WHAT IS SEEN, BUT ON WHAT IS UNSEEN. FOR WHAT IS SEEN IS TEMPORARY, BUT WHAT IS UNSEEN IS ETERNAL.
>
> *2 Corinthians 4:16-18*

WHEN GOD FEELS DISTANT

Where are you, God? I trusted You, and You abandoned me! In our daily sufferings, God can feel distant. After months of unemployment, you may wonder why God seems absent and why He is not providing opportunities for you to work. After losing a loved one, you may struggle when people say that your loved one is with the Lord. You feel a deep separation from your loved one and long to be with them again. Since your loved one feels so far away, so does God. You cannot seem to find comfort, even in prayer or reading His Word.

If you have ever felt abandoned by God amid your suffering, you are not alone. Throughout history, men and women have expressed similar feelings, some of which have been permanently recorded in Scripture. In the book of Psalms, for example, the sons of Korah cried out against God and asked, "Why are you sleeping, God? Why do you hide your face?" In the midst of their trouble, their pain felt unquestionably real, while God seemed to be absent.

Or perhaps, in your suffering, God does not feel far off. He feels like an enemy. Men throughout Scripture also expressed this conclusion (Job 3:1-26, 6:4, Psalm 13, 88, Jeremiah 20:7-18). In Lamentations 3, the author even cried out against God, saying, "He has weighed me down with chains... He blocks out my prayer... He is a bear waiting in ambush, a lion in hiding" (Lamentations 3:7-8, 10). Maybe in your grief, God does feel like a living Father who is lovingly embracing you in His arms. He feels like a smearing, cynical, and condemning judge.

In our suffering, God can feel far because we cannot see what He is doing. We know that God is good, but what is happening in our lives does not feel good. But while emotions scream loudly in our pain, we must actively meditate on what is true by clinging to the promises of Scripture. The faith to trust God comes from His Word. God's Word tells us that He will use everything for our good, even our suffering (Romans 8:28). We may not know why God allows certain losses to occur or why things happen as they do, but we know that God is in control, and He is good. We know that God redeems every second of our pain for His glory, and He will use it for our good. Furthermore, throughout Scripture, we are told not to be surprised by suffering but to expect it (1 Peter 4:12-19). This world will be full of trials, and your suffering does not mean that God has abandoned you, but He does promise to be with you in your trials.

Because of Jesus, God will never abandon us. When Christ died on the cross that fateful day, He was abandoned by God. He was deserted and left to suffer and die alone. He took on the condemnation our sins deserve. He carried our sins to the grave and took on the full wrath and judgment of God. But praise be to God, the grave could not hold Him. Three days later, Jesus rose from the dead and secured our victory over sin and death. In this act, He secured our standing before God. Now, all who trust in God are adopted into God's family, chosen and dearly loved. They are protected, known, and given an eternal inheritance with Christ in heaven. They become children of the King, given all

> **GOD'S WORD TELLS US THAT HE WILL USE EVERYTHING FOR OUR GOOD,** *even our suffering*

the rights and privileges of a child of God. Jesus was abandoned by God on that dreadful cross so that we will never be. As it says in 1 Peter 3:18, "For Christ also suffered for sins once for all, the righteous for the unrighteous, that he might bring you to God."

Although God may feel far off in our pain, we must remind our hearts of what is true. Especially in seasons of grief, we must speak to ourselves about the reality of God's presence and cling to God's Word. If you are in Christ, take heart. God is not far off. He is near to you in your pain. He is holding you and crying with you. He has not abandoned you. He is with you in your grief.

> BLESSED BE THE GOD AND FATHER OF OUR LORD JESUS CHRIST, THE FATHER OF MERCIES AND THE GOD OF ALL COMFORT. HE COMFORTS US IN ALL OUR AFFLICTION, SO THAT WE MAY BE ABLE TO COMFORT THOSE WHO ARE IN ANY KIND OF AFFLICTION, THROUGH THE COMFORT WE OURSELVES RECEIVE FROM GOD. FOR JUST AS THE SUFFERINGS OF CHRIST OVERFLOW TO US, SO ALSO THROUGH CHRIST OUR COMFORT OVERFLOWS.
>
> *2 Corinthians 1:3-5*

PURPOSELESSNESS IN LIFE

After your loss, you may feel purposeless. You want to climb into the darkness of the casket with your loved one. Playfulness feels irrelevant. You feel useless and depressed. You cannot see any purpose in living.

Perhaps you feel purposeless after loss because your responsibilities in life have changed. You are no longer a wife after the loss of your spouse. You no longer have as many meals to prepare or couples events to attend. Or you may feel empty and direction-less after another month with a negative pregnancy test after years of trying to have a baby. You wish you had babies to rock or noses to wipe, but instead, you sit in your quiet room each night, alone.

While the particulars of your day may change in grief, your ultimate purpose as a child of God remains the same. Your goal in life remains unshakable: to glorify God. He has placed you in a particular season of life with unique trials, but He has not abandoned you or left you without a reason to live. Read the following verses, and underline your purpose according to the Bible:

- *...everyone who bears my name and is created for my glory. I have formed them; indeed, I have made them.* — Isaiah 43:7

- *So, whether you eat or drink, or whatever you do, do everything for the glory of God.* — 1 Corinthians 10:31

- *My eager expectation and hope is that I will not be ashamed about anything, but that now as always, with all courage, Christ will be highly honored in my body, whether by life or by death.* — Philippians 1:20

In your grief, you still have a unique opportunity to make God's glory known to the ends of the earth. In the midst of your pain, you can continue to love those around you, pointing to a strength that comes from God alone. Today's trial becomes an opportunity for you to endure in faith despite your troubles and temptations.

God is with you in your moments of sorrow, and He will work them out for your good. Even though grief may drastically change your life, your purpose remains the same: to glorify God by loving Him and others. He will use you to accomplish His perfect purposes and give you what you need for each day.

> I HAVE TOLD YOU THESE THINGS SO THAT IN ME YOU MAY HAVE PEACE. YOU WILL HAVE SUFFERING IN THIS WORLD. BE COURAGEOUS! I HAVE CONQUERED THE WORLD.
>
> *John 16:33*

DOUBT IN THE LORD'S GOODNESS

As we journey through grief, we often respond in ways that surprise us. Perhaps you were strong in your faith before your loss. You carried a happy demeanor and joyfully loved those around you. You were the first to volunteer and the last to leave church on Sundays as you were engaged in meaningful conversations with other members. But now, despair, anxiety, and doubt have become your closest friends. You feel self-absorbed and struggle with an internal dialogue that, quite frankly, surprises you. You want to hide in a corner and withdraw from the world. You identify closely with Job's wife, perhaps for the first time in your life, who, in the midst of her loss, encouraged her husband to "curse God and die!" (Job 2:9).

Reformer Martin Luther described suffering as having two levels. The first is external, or the painful circumstances of life. The second is internal, or how we respond to the brokenness of life. When tragedy strikes, we each have the opportunity to press into our faith or to pull away. We can cry out to God with honest cries and laments before the Lord, casting all our cares on Him because He cares for us (1 Peter 5:7). Or, we can pull away from God and tumble into greater darkness, pushing against our only source of lasting peace.

God is big enough to handle our questions and doubts. In the book of Habakkuk, the prophet modeled this for us. Facing a world of trouble, He cried out to God asking, "Where are you? Why did you allow such evil to happen?" As he wrestled through doubts and despair, He directed His raw and honest doubts at God, and God responded, not with anger at Habakkuk but with compassion and wisdom. Just like Habakkuk, we too can lament and bring our questions to God, rather than withdrawing from Him. Even when the world is falling apart, we can choose to come to God and remember His covenant faithfulness to His children. God is in control, and He can be trusted.

If you are struggling with your faith or wondering if God is real:

- *Talk to a trusted Christian friend about your doubts, and ask for prayer.*
- *Confide in your pastor for prayer, and ask for help as you walk through this difficult season.*
- *Write a letter to God, confessing your doubts and questions. Ask that He would reveal Himself to you and help you through your doubts.*
- *Be in God's Word daily.*
- *Prioritize community within a Bible-believing local church.*

> **I WILL NEVER LEAVE YOU OR ABANDON YOU.**
>
> *Hebrews 13:5*

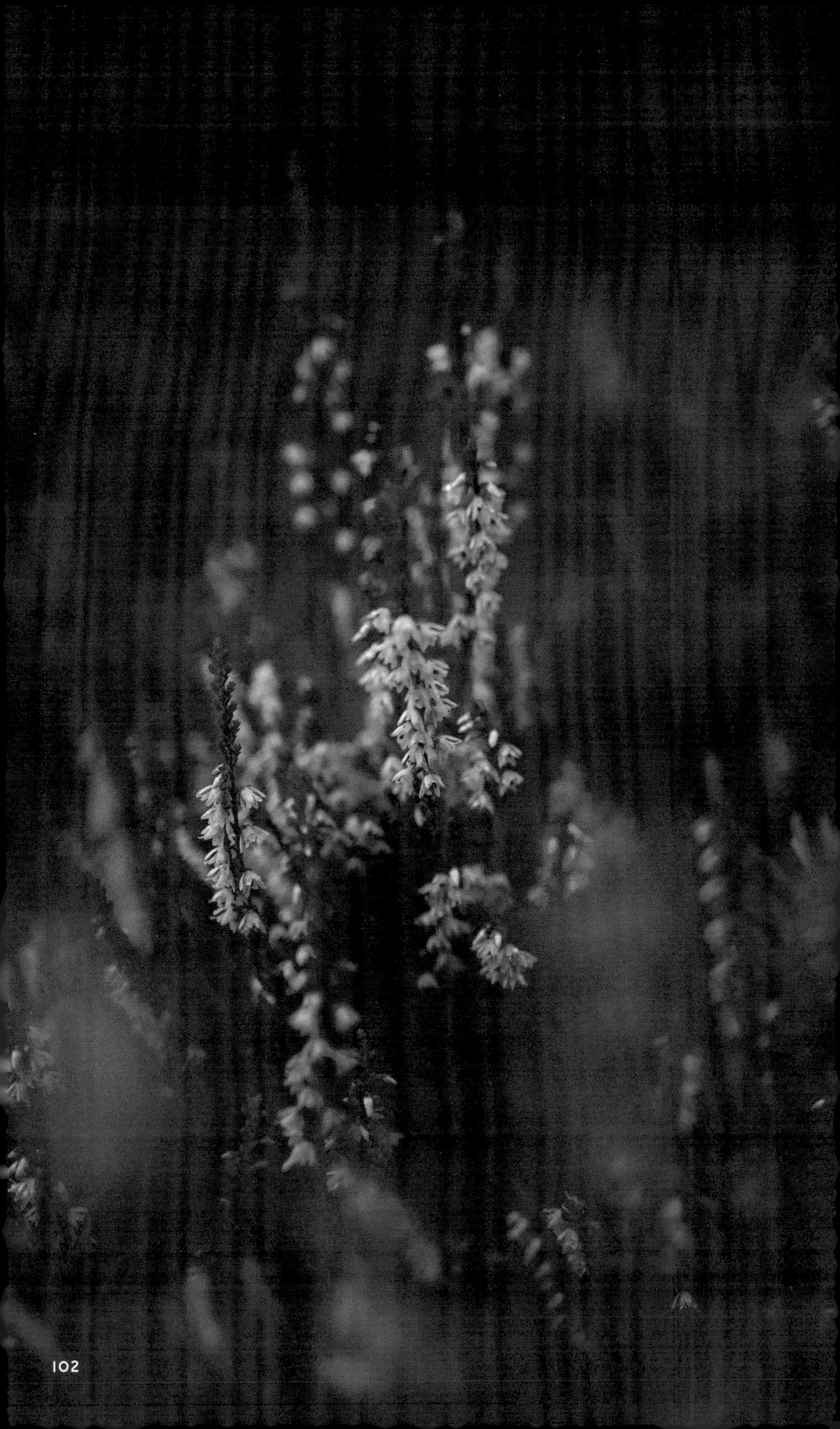

HOPE IN THE LORD

Although it may seem impossible, we can hope in the Lord in every kind of trouble. This hope does not rely on what is seen but on what is unseen. Hope recalls the faithfulness of God in the past and relies on His goodness, even when life does not feel good. It fights to believe what is true and seeks to fear God more than anything else.

The book of Lamentations is an excellent example of this. After the fall of Jerusalem, the people of Israel were killed, tortured, and carried off into exile. The author of the book of Lamentations expressed the emotional and spiritual anguish of this event. He felt physically ill, like his flesh and bones had wasted away (Lamentations 3:4). He felt like the Lord had forsaken him (Lamentations 3:8), blocked his path and surrounded him with massive, inescapable walls (Lamentations 3:9). He felt like an arrow had been driven through his kidneys (Lamentations 3:13) and like he was the laughing stock of everyone (Lamentations 3:14). He felt like the Lord had caused these terrors and was not coming to his rescue. But in the middle of this pain, he also remembered the Lord's faithful love and mercies. He chose to wait on the salvation of the Lord and put his hope in Him, saying:

> *Yet I call this to mind, and therefore I have hope: Because of the Lord's faithful love we do not perish, for his mercies never end. They are new every morning; great is your faithfulness! I say, "The Lord is my portion, therefore I will put my hope in him." The Lord is good to those who wait for him, to the person who seeks him. It is good to wait quietly for salvation from the Lord (Lamentations 3:21-26).*

Just as the author of Lamentations actively recalled and hoped in the Lord, we can do this too. It is possible to trust God, even when we do not understand His ways. This kind of hope does not hide its pain, wearing a plastered smile and parroting to others that "everything is fine." Instead, hope waits for something greater, even amid our pain. Hope relies on the faithful love of God and remembers that God will one day comfort every pain and heal every wound. He will give us the grace we need for each day and sustain us through our trials. As we depend on Him, He gives us a living hope that endures even the worst of life's trials. He will wipe away every tear and right every wrong. As we hope in the Lord, we remember that we are not alone and that He is coming again.

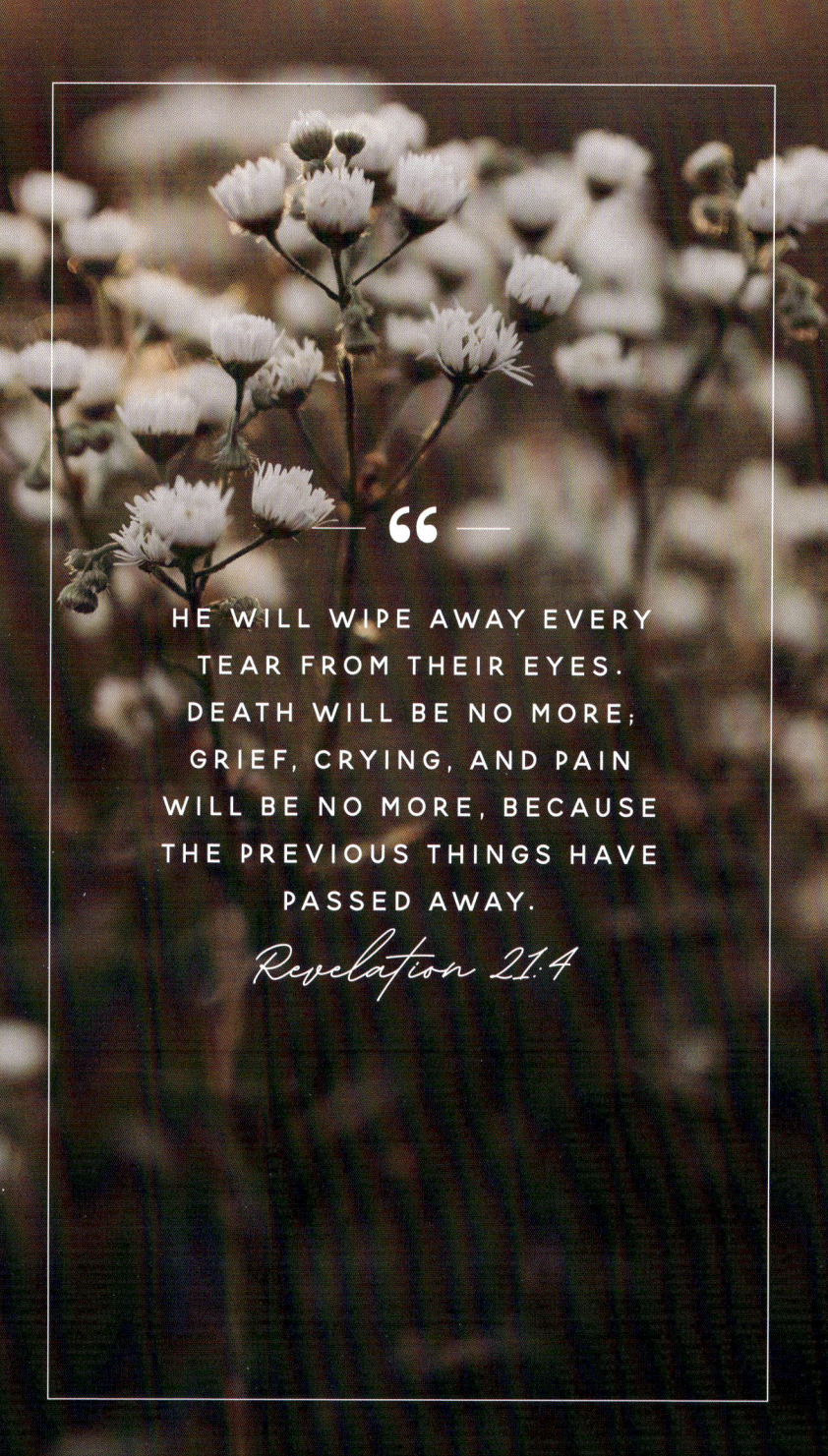

> "HE WILL WIPE AWAY EVERY TEAR FROM THEIR EYES. DEATH WILL BE NO MORE; GRIEF, CRYING, AND PAIN WILL BE NO MORE, BECAUSE THE PREVIOUS THINGS HAVE PASSED AWAY.
>
> *Revelation 21:4*

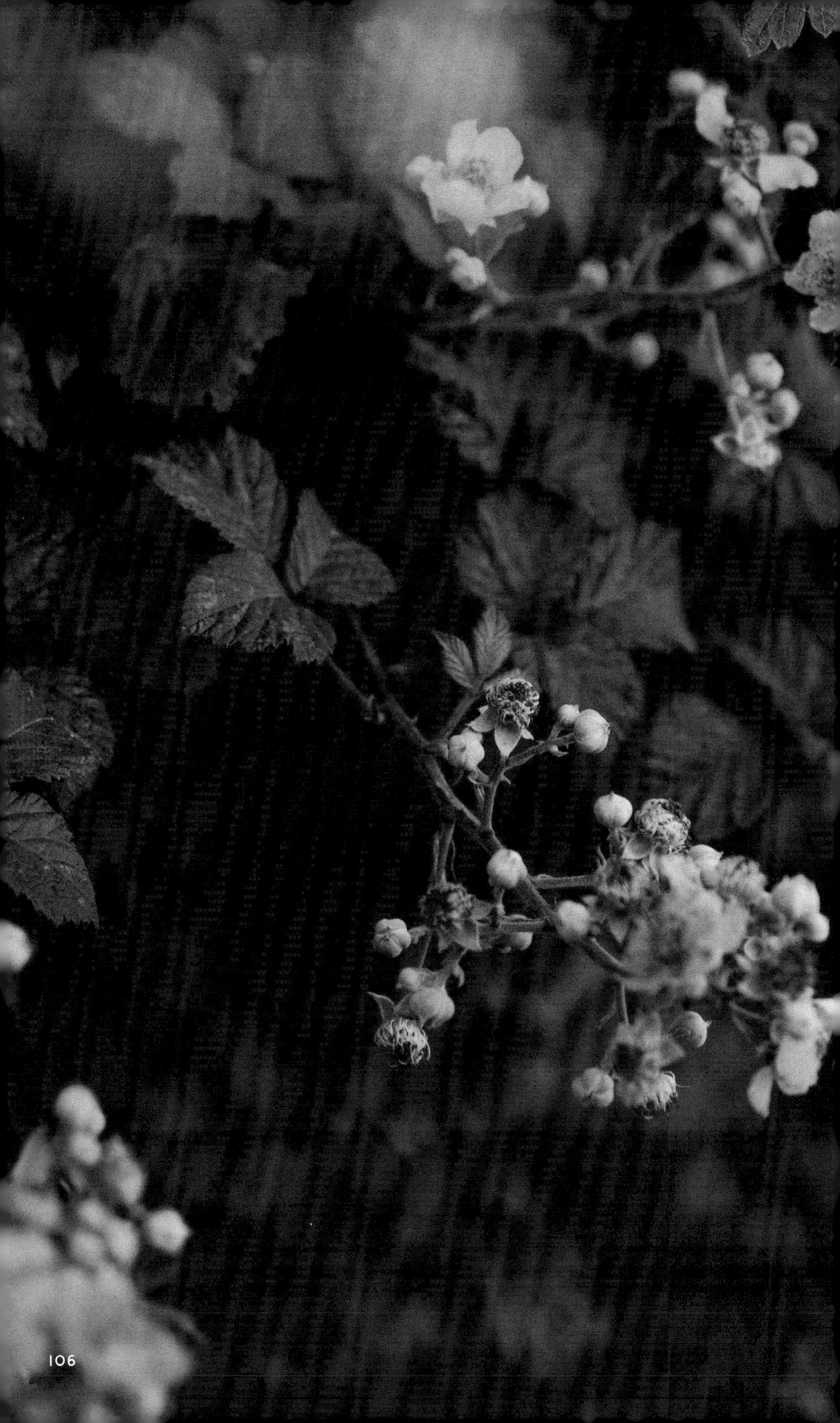

—06—

HOW TO GRIEVE

Acknowledge Your Loss
Cry Out to the Lord
Be Honest with Your Emotions
Understand Your Story
Grieve with Hope
Identify New Goals
Plan for Special Events
Remembering Your Loved Ones
Find Community
Cling to Scripture

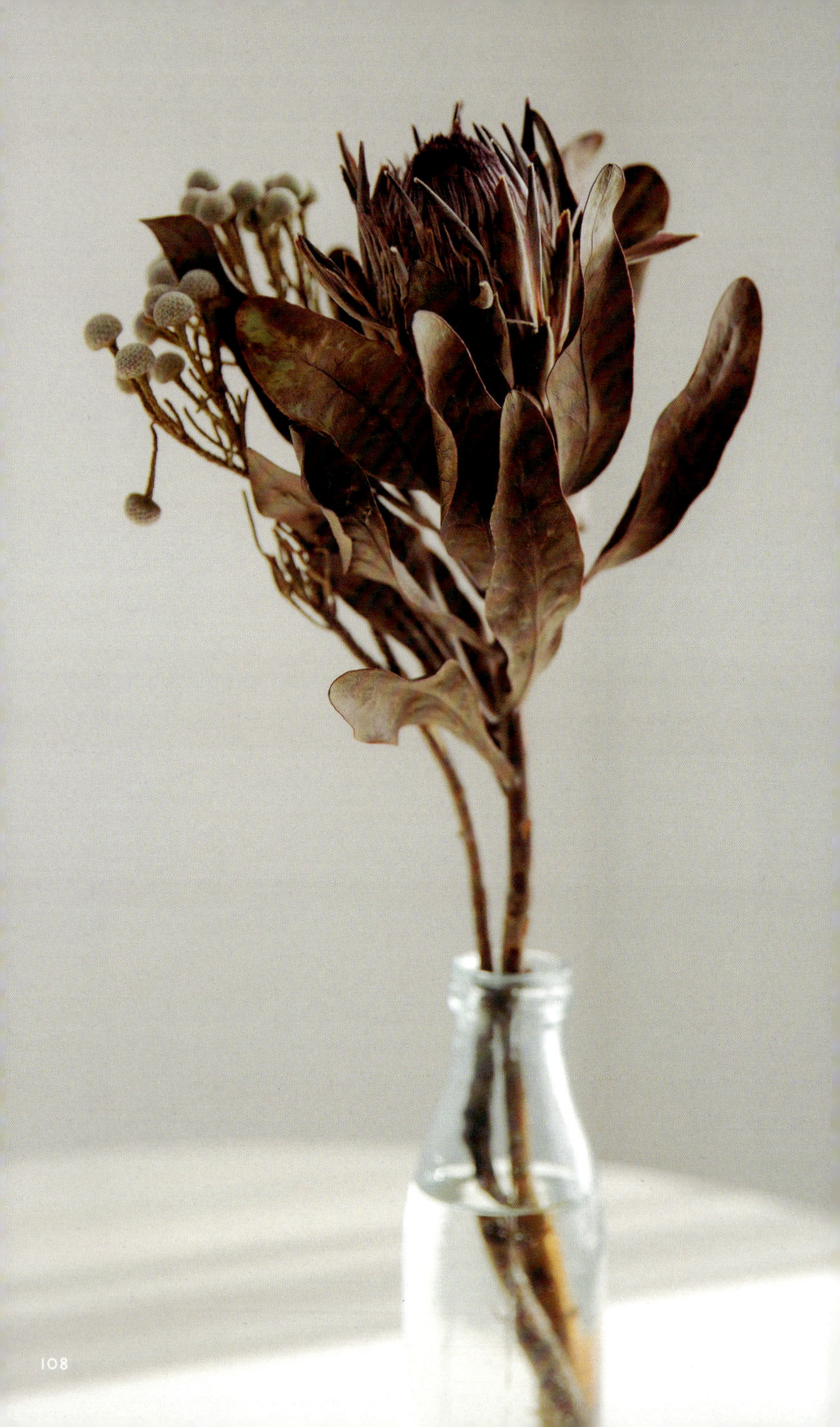

ACKNOWLEDGE YOUR LOSS

A period of denial in grief is normal. God often provides an emotional buffer of protection in the days immediately following a loss, but eventually, our shock will begin to fade. When this happens, we may find ourselves clinging to the normalcy of the past, desperate to avoid reality. We may experience weeks, months, or years of emotional paralyzation. Maybe you feel stuck, not knowing how to move forward in a world that was changed by a single event. Life stopped for you the moment you experienced loss but now seems to continue irreverently for the rest of the world. Maybe you have difficulty referring to your loved one in the past tense because it would mean that your loss really happened. You do not want to acknowledge the loss because then you would be forced to move forward in life without your loved one.

Our grief makes us feel powerless in a dangerous world. It shows us our limits and reminds us that we are not in control. Although we may initially face loss with denial, in time, we must acknowledge the loss in order to find healing. As we enter into the present, we acknowledge that God is there to meet us. He will comfort us and provide the grace we need for each moment. As we face our new realities, we remember that God is with us. He is our help. We do not need to avoid our difficult emotions or resist sadness. He will comfort us through them. Though we do not know why our loss has happened, we trust that God is still in control, and He is still good.

Even if it may seem impossible, God will help you as you grieve. He is with you in your sorrow, and He will provide the hope, grace, and faith that you need. He will give you the grace to face hard emotions and walk through the difficult journey of grief.

Acknowledging Your Loss

I call to you from the ends of the earth
when my heart is without strength.
Lead me to a rock that is high above me,
for you have been a refuge for me,
a strong tower in the face of the enemy.

PSALM 61:2-3

Use these pages to process your loss, including the actual event, as well as how you are responding physically, emotionally, and spiritually.

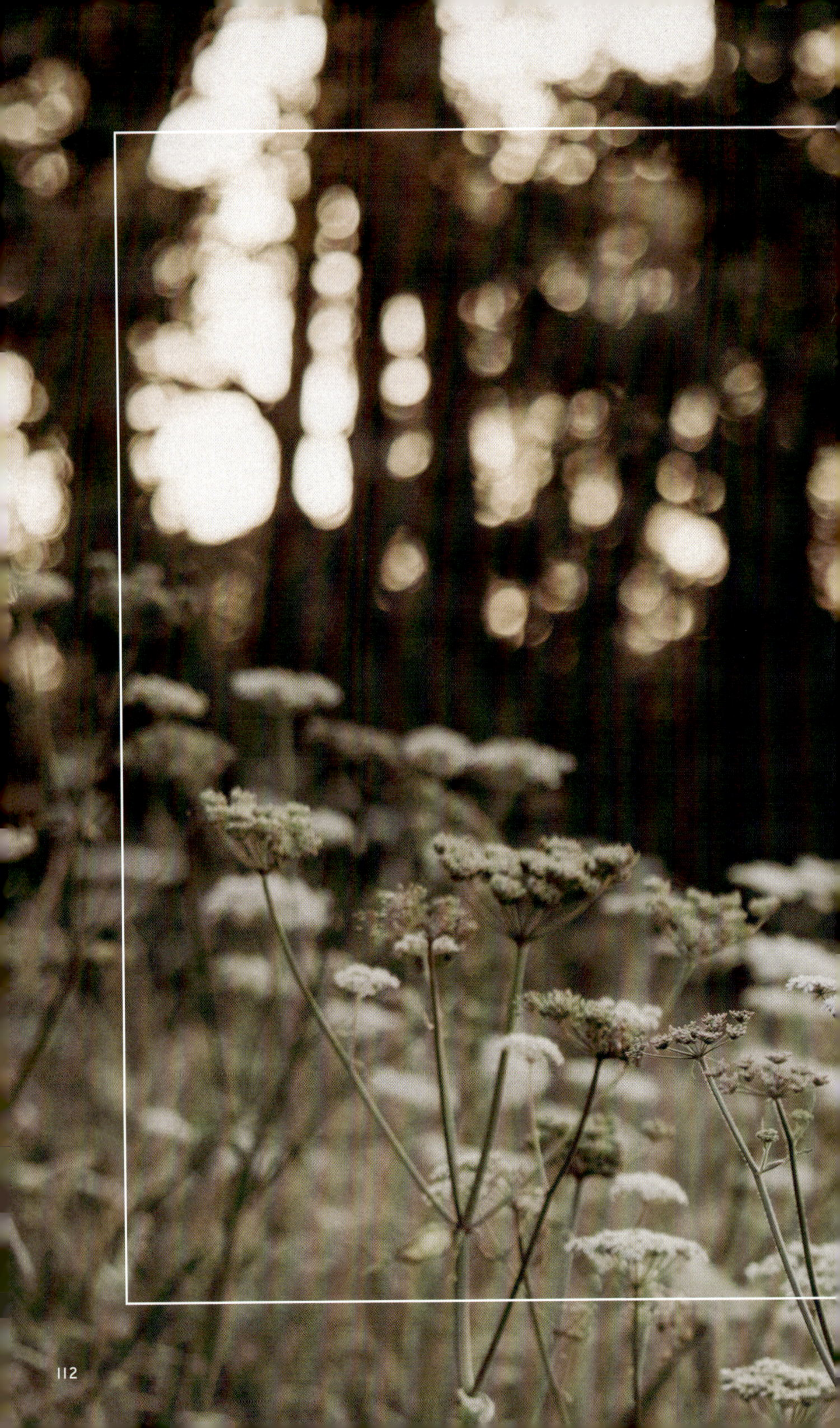

> THOUGH WE DO NOT KNOW WHY OUR LOSS HAS HAPPENED, WE TRUST THAT GOD IS STILL IN CONTROL, AND *He is still good*

CRY OUT TO THE LORD

When you are grieving, prayer can be hard. Your words drag like heavy boots trudging through thick mud. It feels impossible to pray to a God who could have stopped your loss from happening. You feel guilty, angry, afraid, and empty.

Although prayer can be difficult in grief, remember that God is with you always. He desires to comfort you and bring healing to your soul. He will help you in your time of need. He is not surprised by your emotions or questions. He knows it all. He knows when we are angry with Him and when we are too tired to eat. He knows when we cannot hold a thought in our minds and when our fears are overwhelming. He knows it all, and He does not want you to feel alone in your grief. He invites you to cry out to Him in the midst of every emotion, as your very present help in time of need (Psalm 46:1). He is the only One who can provide real and lasting peace for our souls.

Not only this, prayer is a gift to the suffering believer. Through prayer, we lay our burdens before the Lord and express our deepest pains. We receive God's peace and help and find comfort for our souls. Charles Spurgeon, an influential pastor in England in the 1800s, experienced this grace firsthand. Despite his powerful preaching and growing fame, he also battled regular seasons of depression, difficulty, and loss. He was familiar with the pain and heavy burdens of life. In the midst of this, he said, "In all states of dilemma or of difficulty, prayer is an available source. The ship of prayer may sail through all temptations, doubts and fears, straight up to the throne of God; and though she may be outward bound with only griefs, and groans, and sighs, she shall return freighted with a wealth of blessings!" In prayer, we find the comfort, peace, and help we need.

If you cannot find the words to pray, use the words of Scripture to help you. Read the Psalms back to God, inserting your own story as you pray. Tell God how you feel, and ask for His help. Ask Him your questions, and tell Him your doubts. As you acknowledge your loss, cry out to the Lord for help. Our God understands our pain and sorrow, and He is acquainted with our grief. He understands our pain and intercedes for us in prayer. He is our closest friend and companion, our refuge and fortress.

> ALTHOUGH PRAYER CAN BE DIFFICULT IN GRIEF, REMEMBER THAT *God is with you always*

Prayer Journaling

Read Psalm 69. Take note of the psalmist's:

- *Desperate plea to the Lord for help (verses 1, 14, 29)*
- *Exhaustive and overwhelming circumstances (verses 1-3)*
- *Relational problems (verses 4, 8-12, 21-28)*
- *Remembrance of the Lord's character and faithfulness (verses 5, 13, 16, 29-36)*

Despite great loss and overwhelming circumstances, the psalmist cried out to the Lord and remembered His steadfast love. After reading this psalm, personalize it, and pray these words back to the Lord.

BE HONEST WITH YOUR EMOTIONS

The goal of grieving well is to learn how to find hope in our sadness, not to escape grief or schedule it within predictable boundaries. As we move past denial and enter into the present, we experience God's very present help for us. When we acknowledge our emotions, we have the opportunity to apply the hope of Scripture to them. For example, if we are struggling with fear, we can find God's comforting assurance that He is with us when we are afraid (Isaiah 41:10). If we are struggling with anger, we can read the Bible to see what it says about anger with God (Psalm 22) or anger with others (Matthew 18:21-35). The Lord invites us to pour out our emotions to Him and ask for His help. We can find comfort in the words of Job, Habakkuk, and David as they experience the range of human emotions and continue to place their faith in God.

Do not rush or ignore your grief. Rather, press into the Lord in prayer and find God's hope for your soul through His Word.

> "
> THE LORD INVITES US TO POUR OUT OUR EMOTIONS TO HIM AND *ask for His help*

Emotions and the Word

Prayerfully identify 2-3 emotions you have experienced recently. Then examine the Scriptures to see what it says about these thoughts and feelings.

EMOTION	SCRIPTURE
ANGER	Psalm 22, James 1:20, Ephesians 4:26, Matthew 18:21-35
SADNESS	Psalm 6, 2 Corinthians 1:3, Psalm 27
JEALOUSY	Psalm 37:1-3, Proverbs 23: 17-18, 1 Peter 2:1-3
FEAR	Psalm 23, Philippians 4:8, Isaiah 41:10
PURPOSELESSNESS IN SUFFERING	John 16:33, Romans 8:28

Which emotions have you experienced most strongly throughout your grieving journey? What (if anything) has kept you from acknowledging these emotions or bringing them before the Lord in prayer?

_____
_____
_____

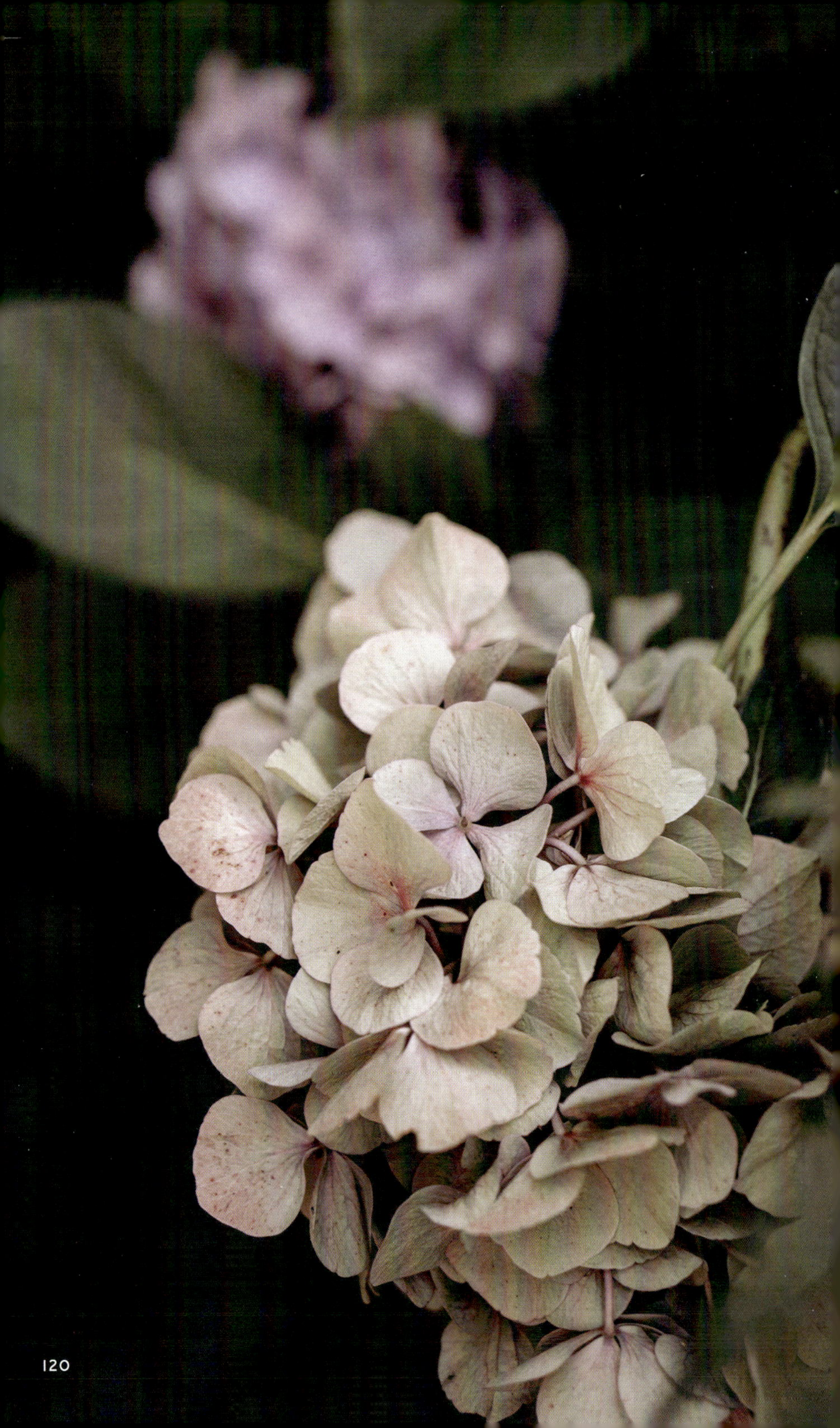

UNDERSTAND YOUR STORY

In grief, we often want to understand the "why." Why did this happen? Why was I fired? Why did he leave me? Why did she die? Although God may not answer all of our "why" questions on this side of heaven, we know that God uses every trial to refine us for His glory and our good (Romans 8:28). Read 1 Peter 1:3-9 as it speaks about suffering:

> *Blessed be the God and Father of our Lord Jesus Christ. Because of his great mercy he has given us new birth into a living hope through the resurrection of Jesus Christ from the dead and into an inheritance that is imperishable, undefiled, and unfading, kept in heaven for you. You are being guarded by God's power through faith for a salvation that is ready to be revealed in the last time. You rejoice in this, even though now for a short time, if necessary, you suffer grief in various trials so that the proven character of your faith—more valuable than gold which, though perishable, is refined by fire—may result in praise, glory, and honor at the revelation of Jesus Christ. Though you have not seen him, you love him; though not seeing him now, you believe in him, and you rejoice with inexpressible and glorious joy, because you are receiving the goal of your faith, the salvation of your souls.*

When Peter wrote this letter, his audience was familiar with loss. They lived in exile: persecuted, mocked, maligned, and unjustly discriminated against because of their faith in Christ. Their Christian friends and family members received the same treatment, being insulted, mocked, and possibly even beaten for following Jesus (1 Peter 2:20).

As a people, they had endured great loss. Can you imagine the disappointment of being exiles in a foreign land? The hopes and dreams deferred as family members were hurt in mob violence? The pain of holidays altered as family members were imprisoned for wrongs they did not even commit? Even so, Peter called the people to rejoice, knowing that God had purposes beyond what they could see.

The Apostle Peter would prove this point with his life, eventually being killed for his faith in Jesus (John 21:18-19). Tradition says he asked to be crucified upside down on a cross because he did not feel worthy to die in the same way as his Savior. Peter trusted that his suffering was not the end of his story. He knew that God was weaving a masterpiece, redeeming and using every loss for His grander purposes.

In light of the cross, we can also grieve with hope. We can rejoice even in our trials, knowing that the proven character of our faith will result in praise, glory, and honor at the revelation of Jesus (1 Peter 1:3). We can praise God because we have an inheritance that is unattainable, unfading, and undefiled (1 Peter 1:4). We can worship God because we are guarded by His power (1 Peter 1:5). This does not mean that we do not feel sad. Rather, it means we can find hope, even in our sorrow, because we remember that God is using every painful circumstance for good.

Like Peter, we know that suffering is not the end of our story. We believe that God will use every minute of our pain for His glory and our good (Hebrews 5:8, Romans 8:28, James 1:3-4). He may use our losses to strengthen our relationship with God (Romans 8:17-18), reveal existing sin (John 15:22), grow our affections for Christ, or increase our longing for heaven (1 Peter 1:3-9). He may allow us to minister to someone with similar struggles (2 Corinthians 1:3-4) or bear witness to the surpassing greatness of God, even in the midst of our pain (2 Corinthians 4:7-8). But, even when we do not see His plan, we trust in faith that God is working through our loss. Our pain is not meaningless. Through it, God is doing something grander than we could ever imagine.

> WE BELIEVE THAT GOD WILL USE EVERY MINUTE OF OUR PAIN *for His glory and our good*

A Timeline of Your Loss

On the following timeline, mark your loss in the middle of the line. Write down key events that happened before your loss, as well as significant events that have happened or are expected to happen after the event. Mark key moments when you have seen God's faithfulness in your life.

The goal of this exercise is to help you remember God's faithfulness throughout your life. If you are in Christ, your life is defined by more than a single event, as significant as this event was. Your life has been redeemed by God, purchased by the blood of Christ. You have been adopted into God's family and protected as a child of the King. God has not abandoned you, even in the midst of significant loss. He will use this loss for His glory and your good. He will restore every loss and heal every hurt. He has been faithful to you in the past, and He will be faithful to you in the future. When we see Him face to face, there will be no more tears, hurting, or pain (Revelation 21:1-4). We long for this day while remembering His faithfulness to us in the past.

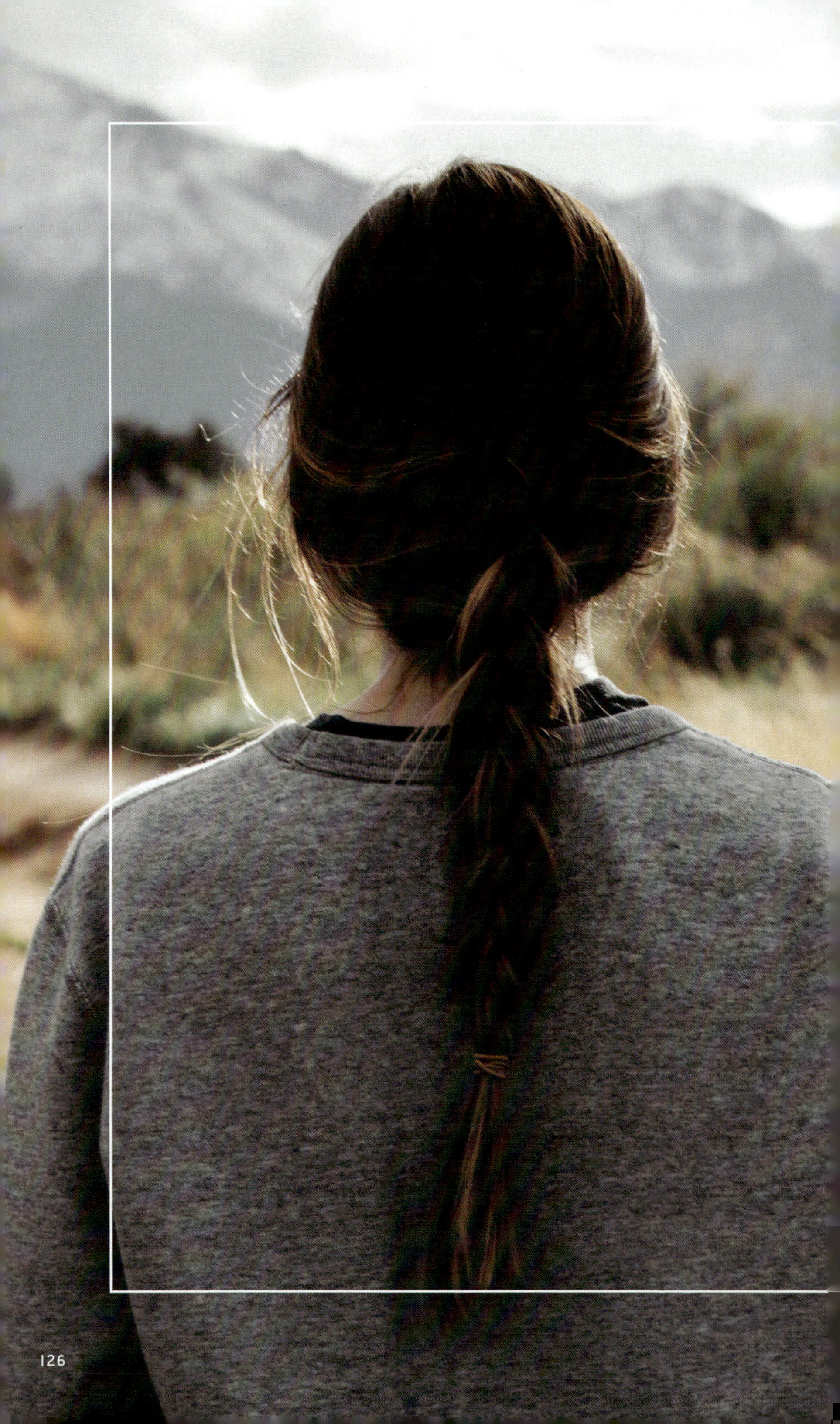

> WE BELIEVE THAT
> GOD WILL USE EVERY
> MINUTE OF OUR PAIN
> *for His glory*
> AND OUR GOOD.

GRIEVE WITH HOPE

In Scripture, we are called to grieve with hope (1 Thessalonians 4:13). While this verse may seem impossible at first, it is also comforting — for within it, it acknowledges that we grieve. God knows that we are in pain and is with us in our loss. We can freely grieve before our all-knowing and compassionate God, not hiding any of our emotions from Him but bringing them all before our Father in prayer. We can rage against the brokenness of the world and lament our loss. We can mourn as we are honest with our emotions and face our grief.

So then, what does it look like to grieve with hope? How can we continue our grieving journey, identifying glimpses of grace and moving forward in the peace that God provides? We can have hope because we know that God will make all things right. Even when life seems unbearable, we have a God who loves us unconditionally and is powerful over all. In our suffering, we can "count it all joy" because we know that God is with us, working through our pain and redeeming it all for good (James 1:3-4). If you lost a loved one who trusted in Jesus, you can grieve knowing that your separation is only momentary. You will see your loved one again in heaven, with renewed bodies and eternal joy. On the other hand, if you experience uncertainties about your loved one's faith, unanswered questions, or unresolved injustices, you can trust that God is working for your good in every hurt, loss, and sorrow. He does what is perfect. He will make all things right. He is doing something through our sorrow, a work of eternal significance and purpose. We may not see it now, but one day when He returns, He will make all things clear. He will right every wrong and heal every hurt. He will come to make all things new.

But perhaps you still find it difficult to grieve with hope. Consider taking one of the following steps to continue to process your loss and find the peace that God provides:

- *Make a list of unfinished business. Is there anything you can do to honor your loved one or process your grief? Can you make a list of regrets from your job or lessons to remember for next time? Can you leave a letter at the gravesite or say sorry to someone you hurt?*

- *Use art, writing, or other creative means to express what is difficult to verbally communicate your loss.*

- *If there is unfinished business that you cannot address, surrender it to the Lord, and remember that He is in control. Forgive the ones who have hurt you, and trust that God is the just judge. He sees all, and He will right every wrong.*

- *Write down a list of God's attributes. How do they bring you comfort?*

- *Read Revelation 21. How does the end of the story encourage you in your current suffering?*

- *Write a goodbye letter. Include what you will miss about your loved one, what you remember doing with that person, and how you are adjusting to life without him or her.*

> "
> WE CAN HAVE HOPE BECAUSE
> WE KNOW THAT GOD WILL
> *make all things right*

Writing a Goodbye Letter

Writing goodbye letters can be a helpful way to find closure, process lingering regrets, and express longing. Feel free to do this for other types of loss like losing a job or a home. Read this goodbye letter to a loved one as an example.

Dear [name],

I miss you. I can't believe you're gone. Sometimes, this doesn't feel real. It feels like a bad dream, a nightmare really. I think about all the times we had together, and I want more of them. I want more memories, as I desperately hold on to the ones I have. It wasn't supposed to be this way.

And at the same time, in the past few months, I've been slowly learning how to live without you. I've been learning how to trust God, even when life doesn't make sense. He's been taking care of me throughout this painful and unexpected roller coaster of grief. I'm learning how to live with this hole in my heart and smile again. I'm learning not to feel guilty if I don't cry every hour because I know you wouldn't want me to dwell in my sadness, refusing joy forever because you're gone. But I still miss you and am learning how to live without you.

You were such a blessing to my life. I think about you everyday. Even as I move forward and let you go, I'm so thankful for all the times we've had together. Life will never be the same without you, and I will never forget you. Thank you for all the joy you brought to my life. Thank you for everything. I miss you forever, and I love you always.

Love,
[name]

Use the section below to write a goodbye letter to the person or thing that you have lost. You can personalize this to a lost loved one, dream, job, health condition, loss of innocence, or any other form of loss.

Dear _____.

_____

_____

_____

_____

_____

_____

_____

_____

_____

_____

_____

_____

_____

_____

Love,

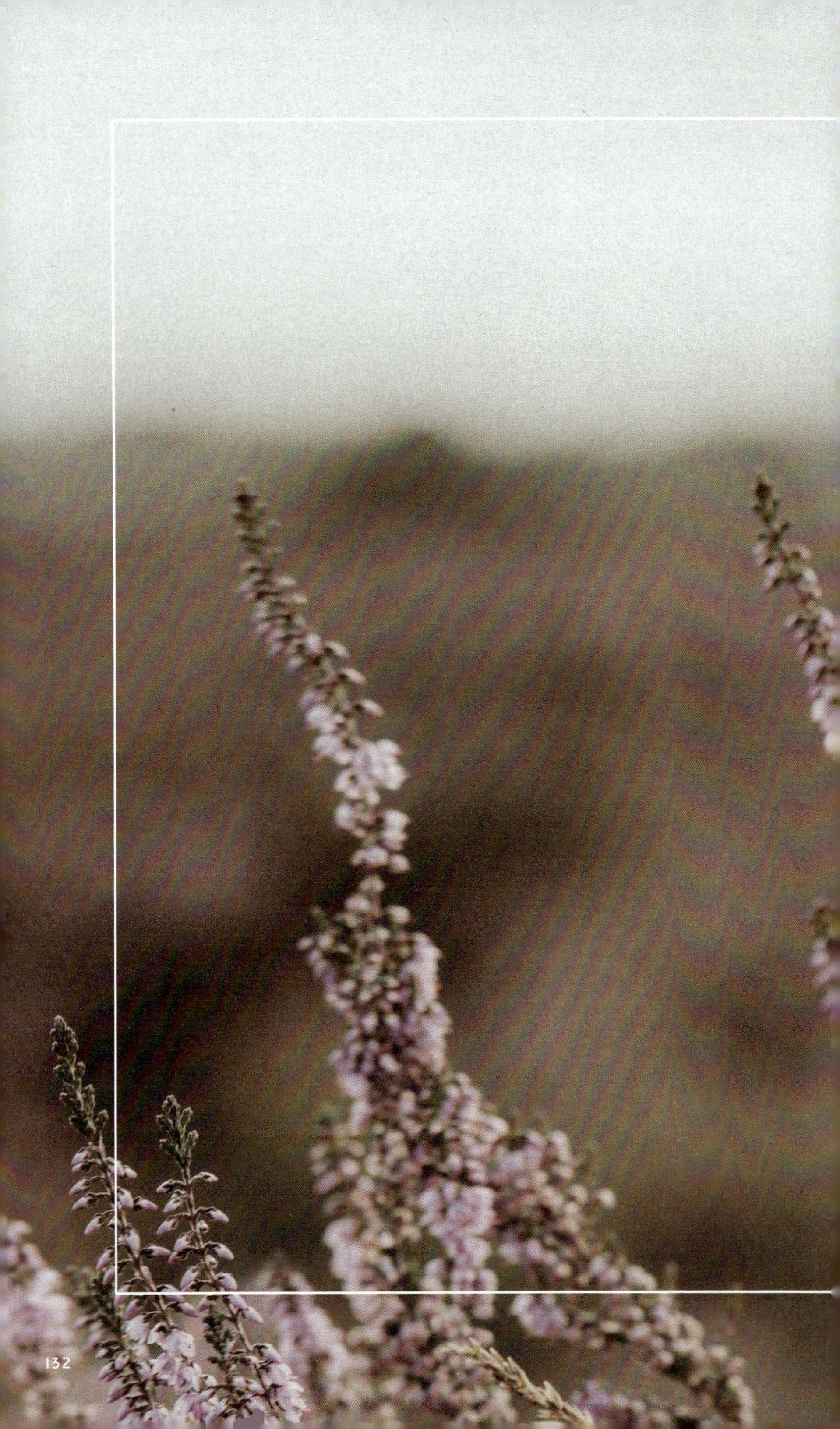

> EVEN WHEN LIFE SEEMS UNBEARABLE, WE HAVE A GOD WHO *loves us unconditionally* AND IS POWERFUL OVER ALL.

IDENTIFY NEW GOALS

Your appetite has returned. You are looking forward to next week. You have started to laugh at jokes again, and you occasionally experience peace, even within your grief spasms. You feel as if you are entering into a new season, the pain still present, yet you are cognizant of God's grace in the day-to-day.

To preface, this section may not be suitable for fresh grief. There is a season to mourn, lament, and cry. As we have discussed, it is normal to experience grief's physical, emotional, and spiritual effects. We should not rush or hide it. When appropriate, though, we can slowly begin to identify new goals in our daily schedules. We learn to recognize what activities bring life and how to spend our time. We press into the ordinary means of grace and rely on Christ in our grief. We remember the old rhythms that were helpful to us before our loss, and we endure in our habits of faith. As we continue our grieving journey, we learn to identify new goals and ways of living.

Consider the following case study as you create new plans or goals after loss:

> *Joseph was one of the twelve sons of Jacob (Genesis 37-50). He was favored by his dad but hated by his brothers. One day, his brothers were so bothered by him that they wanted to kill him. They settled for selling him into slavery and pretending he was dead. Years later, he advanced in his new land and became successful, but he was falsely accused of abuse and thrown into jail. Then, he was forgotten in jail by those who promised to help him. Yet, throughout each stage, Joseph was shown God's favor. While a young slave in Egypt, he advanced within the ranks of the foreign palace. From the jail, he was trusted by the prison guard. Finally, when freed from prison, he became the pharaoh's second-in-command. In each season, Joseph*

had to learn new purposes and goals while mourning the betrayal and loss he had experienced.

Many years later, when Joseph was reunited with his brothers, he showed remarkable wisdom and grace. Because of his position in the pharaoh's household, Joseph had the power to save his family from famine. He even told his brothers, "You planned evil against me; God planned it for good to bring about the present result—the survival of many people" (Genesis 50:20). Though his brothers had treated him wrongly, Joseph recognized that God used everything for his good, even his brothers' betrayal.

While Joseph endured much loss, he learned to work hard and identify new goals within his current situation. While acknowledging his loss, he surrendered it to the Lord and did the next task set before him. In our own seasons of grief, it will likely take time to think about the future and to focus on today. But in time, we too can learn to acknowledge our loss, surrender it to the Lord, and do the next thing set before us. We learn to trust God, even when we do not understand. And we learn to find purpose in each new stage of life.

> *We learn to trust God*
> EVEN WHEN WE DO NOT UNDERSTAND

Diagnostic Questions

If you are currently unemployed or are experiencing grief due to the loss of a job, consider these diagnostic questions.

EVALUATE THE PAST

Process your past work experience.

_____

_____

_____

What went well?

_____

_____

_____

What could be improved? *(This could include areas of personal improvement or evaluating desires for future employment.)*

_____

_____

_____

How was God faithful in your past work experience?

_____

_____

_____

EVALUATE THE PRESENT

Are you faithfully praying to God for wisdom and opportunities?

Who can you ask for advice? Make a list of trusted Christians in your local church, as well as like-minded professionals.

What are your:

    Passions?

    Giftings?

    Opportunities?

Diagnostic Questions

How are you currently growing in your professional skills?

Where are you looking for opportunities or networking connections?

How are you using your season of waiting?

What is God teaching you in this season?

Evaluate your character, competency, and capacity. How can you grow in these areas?

EVALUATE THE FUTURE

If God does not provide in the way that you hope, is He still good?

Goals: What are your short-term and long-term goals?

1 Year Goals

5 Year Goals

20 Year Goals

Look up Matthew 6:33-34. How does this encourage you as you think about the future?

Are you prepared for eternity? Have you trusted in Jesus as your Lord and Savior? At times, God can use seasons of loss to remind us of eternal matters and the hope available to those who trust in Him. *Spend time prayerfully evaluating your priorities in light of eternity.* Where are you looking for opportunities or networking connections?

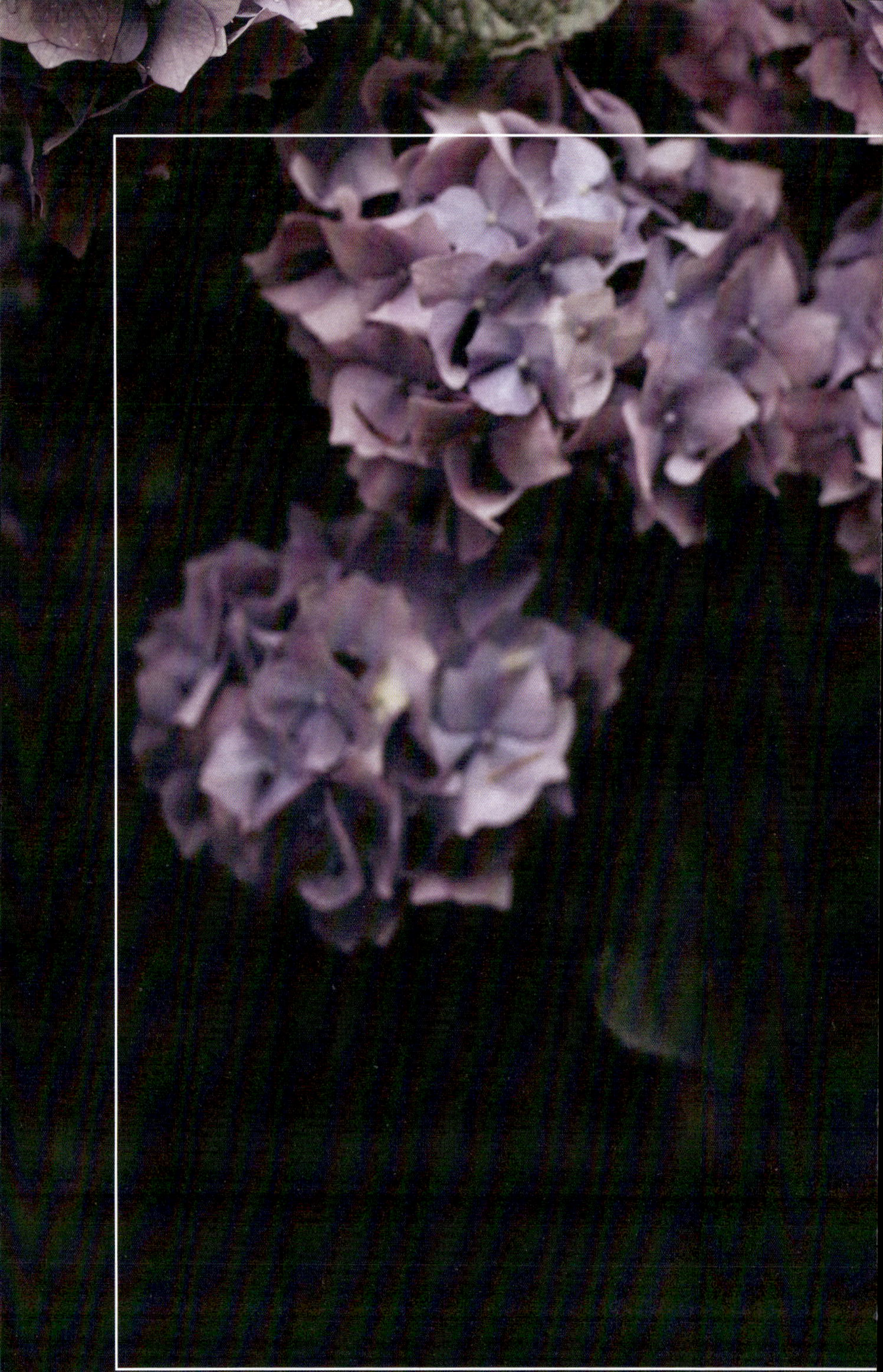

> **AS WE CONTINUE OUR GRIEVING JOURNEY,** *we learn to identify* **NEW GOALS AND WAYS OF LIVING.**

PLAN FOR SPECIAL EVENTS

If you have recently lost a loved one, holidays can be hard. Upcoming birthdays can bring feelings of panic and suffocation. Anniversaries can feel dark and dreadful. As much as possible, plan ahead for these difficult days, and communicate with those around you about how they can help. Identify important dates that you know will be difficult, and write down your desires and expectations for these days in advance. Talk to other people who have experienced grief, and ask about the traditions or practices they have established for difficult days.

As you make new traditions or plans, keep proper expectations. Your plans may change over time. Or you may make a plan and decide to change it at the last minute. That is okay. Remember that your new traditions do not need to be perfect. If the turkey burns or the kids meltdown, remind yourself of the meaning behind these traditions. For example, on the birthday of a deceased loved one, the goal may be to celebrate that person's life by connecting with other family members. In light of this goal, if one family member shows up late or the cake accidentally smashes, it is okay. You can still honor your loved one in the messy moments of the day.

If establishing new holiday traditions seems overwhelming, start with smaller plans. Create a pattern of monthly family dinners, or pray with your kids every night before bed. Once a month, have a family gathering at the park, or text a friend every Tuesday about something you miss about your loved one. Crafting habits in the smaller rhythms of life will help make larger family traditions feel less overwhelming.

For larger holidays, spend time planning and communicating your expectations ahead of time. Intentionally create ways to incorporate your loved one into key holidays. Maybe you take a collective moment of silence before dinner, leave an empty chair to honor their absence, make their favorite meal, or release balloons in special memory. Although these days may be difficult at first, in time, these traditions can become beautiful and joyful ways to honor your loved one.

> *You can still honor your loved one*
> IN THE MESSY MOMENTS OF THE DAY

Creating New Traditions

Spend time evaluating your previous traditions.

What are your current traditions on important dates (anniversaries, birthdays, loss date, holidays, etc.)?

_____
_____
_____
_____
_____

What days are most difficult for you?

_____
_____
_____
_____

How would you like to honor your loved one on those days? As you make these plans, consider who, what, and where.

_____
_____
_____
_____
_____

Who would you like to include in these traditions? Who has been helpful or supportive in your grief journey? Who else is grieving and would appreciate this tradition?

_____

_____

_____

_____

What would you like to do to honor your loved one or celebrate the day? *Is there a special meal you would like to cook or a game you would like to play? Would you like to hang a stocking, keep an empty chair at the table, or have a moment of silence before dinner?*

_____

_____

_____

_____

Where is a special place you can go to remember your loved one?

_____

_____

_____

_____

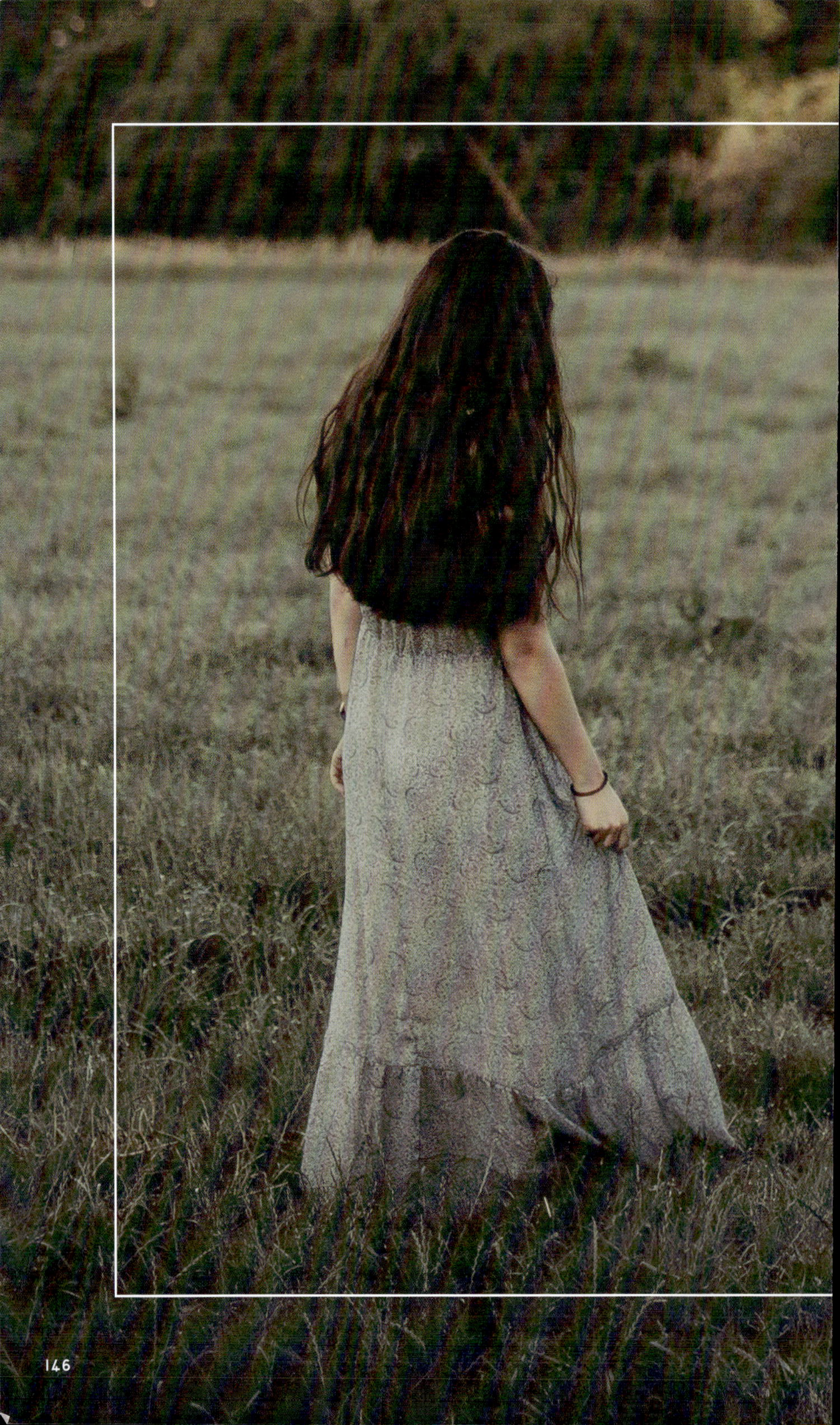

> *Crafting habits in the smaller rhythms of life will help make larger family traditions feel less overwhelming*

REMEMBERING LOVED ONES THROUGH GRIEF

When you lose a loved one, you may feel like their historian. You find yourself telling others about who they were and the life they lived. You want to honor their memory and continue their legacy. In light of this, you may also be afraid that you will forget the details of their life. You do not want to forget her mannerisms in everyday conversations or the look in his eye when he joked.

A helpful tool for the grieving process is active remembering. As we grieve, we remember the good times as well as the hard ones. We do not paint the past with rose-colored glasses, ignoring the weaknesses and troubles of yesterday. Instead, we remember the past with nostalgic honesty. If you recently lost a job, for example, you begin to see the past with a realistic outlook. You remember the moments of being hired, the exhilarating moments of professional success, as well as the conflict in the lunchroom. If you lost a baby in early pregnancy, you remember the hopes, the fears, and the baby names you once pondered. You enter into the present reality, remembering that if God was with you in the pains of yesterday, He will also be with you today.

As you strive to remember your loved one you have lost and share the memories with others, consider one of the following tools:

- *Memory Journal:* Create a journal where you can write down memories of your loved one. The memories do not need to be in chronological order or even written in full sentences. This is a space for you to freely record memories from the past. In the beginning, writing these memories may seem like facts on a page rather than a part of your life. You may feel like there is an emotional wall between you and the page. But as we look back on our past experiences, we begin to acknowledge our loss and learn how to walk forward in the hope that God is with us. This will also help alleviate the anxiety that you will forget your loved one and be a sweet comfort to you in the years to come.

- *Memory Box:* If you are responsible for going through your loved one's belongings, set aside special items to save. Create a box to compile special pictures, recipes, and memories that remind you of that person.

- *Physical Item:* Keep an item that reminds you of your loved one. Maybe it is your dad's baseball hat or your mom's necklace. Maybe it is a watch you would like to pass to your children or a baby's hat from the hospital. Physical items can often bring great comfort to remember your loved one.

- *Prompted Journal:* Use a prompted journal to remember your loved one. This journal may include questions like the ones seen in the following extra on page 150. This can also be a beautiful resource to pass on to others, such as grandchildren to help them remember their grandparents. You may find yourself pleasantly surprised to remember new memories with the help of a prompted journal.

- *Scrapbook:* Make a scrapbook, compiling pictures, sayings, and memories of your loved one.

- *Memorial Site:* Even if there is not a physical body, it can be helpful to have a memorial site to remember the loss of a loved one.

- *Website:* Create a website for others to write down their own memories of your loved one. Do not be afraid to talk about your loved ones or publicly remember them. Ask your friends and family to contribute their memories and photos to the site.

Remembering Your Loved One

Use these pages to remember your loved one. As space is limited, continue to process your memories in a separate journal or with a friend.

How would you describe your loved one? *(This can also be applied to the loss of a dream, job, innocence, relationship, etc.)*

_____

_____

_____

What do you miss most about your loved one?

_____

_____

_____

When do you miss your loved one most?

_____

_____

_____

What is your earliest memory of your loved one?

_____

_____

_____

What are some details that describe your loved one *(favorite color, mannerisms, traits, values)?*

What are a few lessons you learned from your loved one?

How did your loved one change your life?

What do you wish you had told your loved one before they died?

How will you honor their memory?

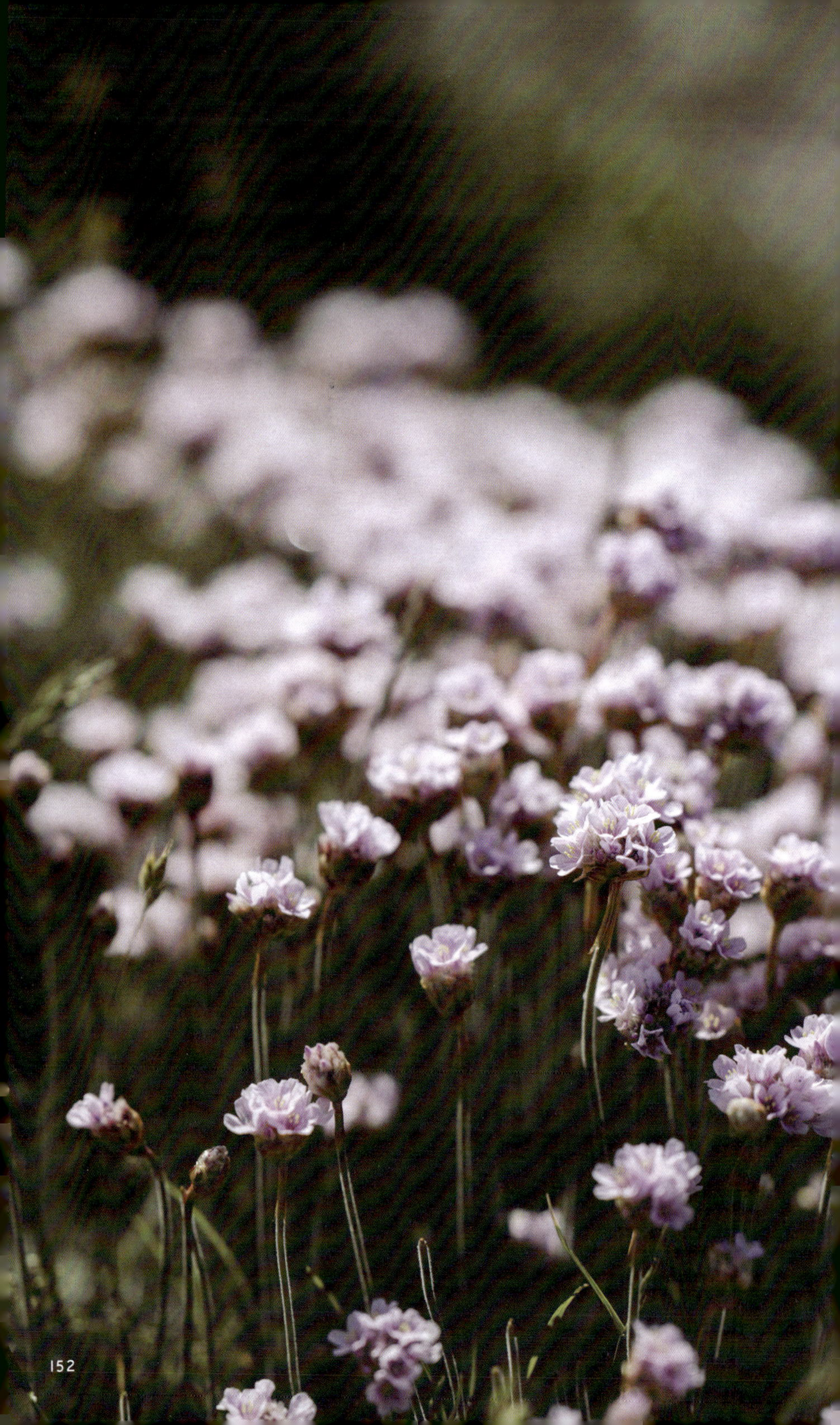

FIND COMMUNITY

When you are grieving, you do not feel like a bubbly, outgoing socialite. You are tired and empty. You want to hide away in your bed, not engage in trivial conversations about paint colors or recipes. Anxiety, mistrust, and despair regularly fill your mind, which might lead you to isolate yourself. Perhaps you experienced a wave of support immediately following your loss, but the visits have since grown more infrequent, and you have found yourself going days without engaging in a meaningful conversation. Or you may feel offended because someone has not acknowledged your loss or asked about your loved one. You think, "They could never understand what I'm feeling," and you decidedly close yourself off from others.

As tempting as it is to isolate yourself in grief, you need community. God does not want you to be alone in your sadness. You do not need to carry this load on your own. He has designed the local church to be a beautiful expression of His care for you.

Keep in mind that those around you may not know how to help you in this season. They may feel awkward and not want to make you sad by reminding you of your loss. If you are silent about your grief, they may even assume that you are fine or that you have moved on. Your friends and family want to be able to love and support you in this season, but they may be clueless about how to do so. As you are able, share your needs with them. Prayerfully identify a few trusted friends with whom you can let your guard down. Let them know how you are doing, and communicate how you are specifically struggling. You may even choose to use an online website to communicate mass updates with your loved ones. Ask for meals or for help choosing a funeral home. Tell them that you love talking about your loved one, and express when you want company or prayer on a difficult day. Ask them to follow up with you each week to see how you are doing. You may even choose to highlight sections of this booklet that you identify with and give it to a friend for better insight into your grieving process.

Support groups can also be a helpful resource in times of grief, as many people find comfort with others who have experienced loss firsthand. Search for a Bible study for those in your life stage or a grief group in your town. Additionally, seek to serve those around you, which will also help you in the grieving process. Though it is difficult, press into a community within your local church where you can be known, loved, cared for, and supported.

Ways to Ask for Help

Asking for help may seem difficult if you are used to living independently. But in grief, you may have difficulty with everyday tasks. As possible, allow others to bless, serve, and love you. Ask for help with:

- *Meals or Groceries: Ask for help in your everyday tasks such as cooking, cleaning, or childcare.*

- *Intermediary for your communications: Sometimes the outpouring of love and support from others can become overwhelming. Ask for help keeping others updated in the midst of your loss. You can use an online platform for this if helpful.*

- *Prayer: Ask for specific prayer requests.*

- *Company: Ask for someone to go for a walk with you or join you for a movie when you feel lonely.*

- *Remembering important facts: If you are struggling with forgetfulness, ask for help remembering important appointments, facts, or events.*

- *Help with logistics: Ask for help identifying a funeral home or watching your children. Ask for help going through your resumé or sorting through your loved one's belongings.*
- *Brainstorming future goals: Ask for help formulating new schedules, goals, or dreams.*
- *Finding a biblical counselor: Ask for help finding a trusted biblical counselor.*

> AS TEMPTING AS IT IS TO ISOLATE YOURSELF IN GRIEF, *you need community*

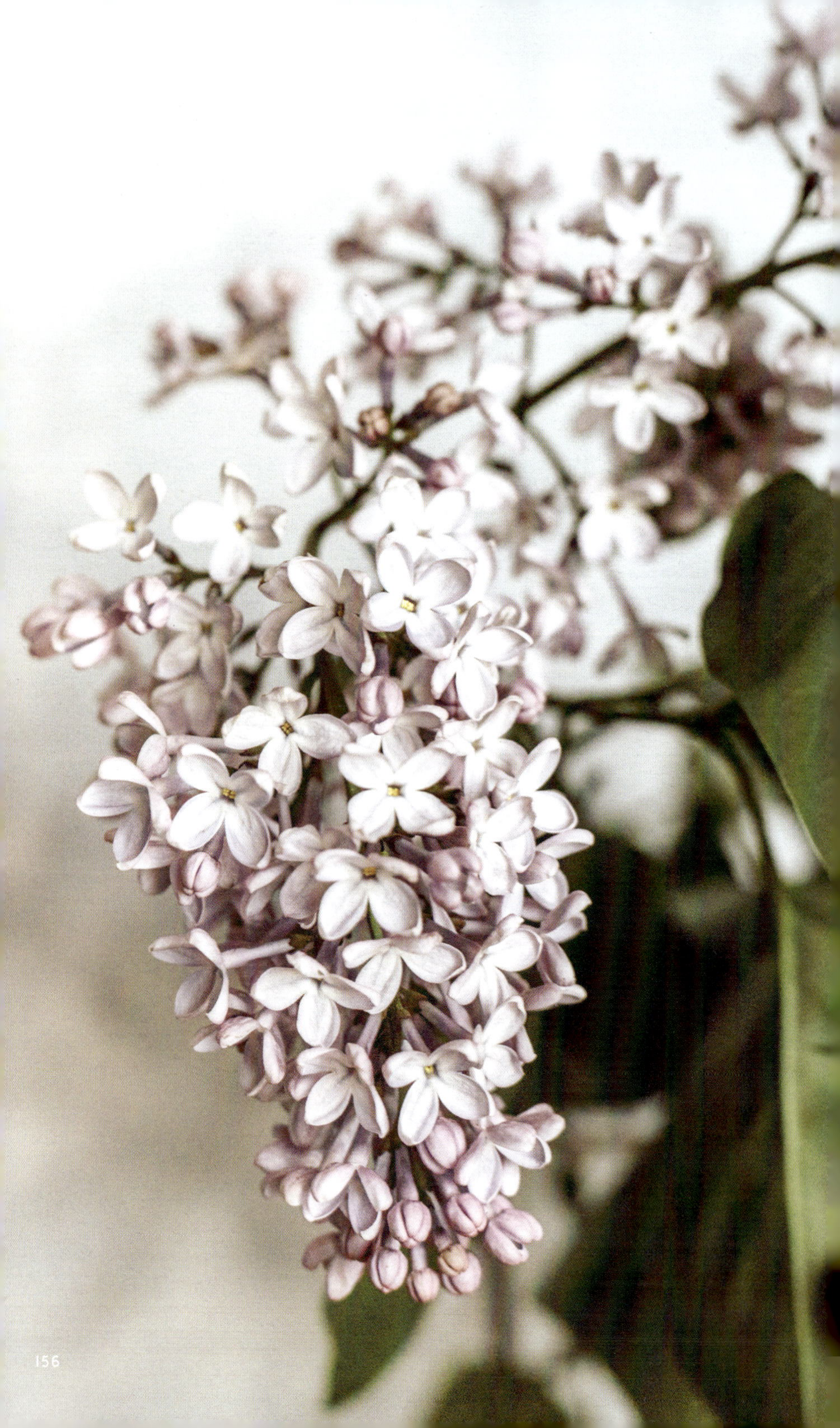

CLING TO SCRIPTURE

In grief, our minds can often feel hazy. Remembering what day it is can seem like a monumental task, let alone recalling deep, theological truths. Thankfully, God knows our frame and is patient with us in every season. He has not left us alone but has given us His Word to cling to as a solid rock on shaky days.

Throughout Scripture, God repetitively reminds His people of the same foundational truths. He is God. He is in control. He is good. He loves us and cares for us. He does not maliciously smirk at our pain, sadistically enjoying our suffering and sanctification. He is not distant or absent. Instead, He enters into our pain with us and carries us through it. Though He is in control of all things, He does not rejoice when we are hurt. He helps us in our weaknesses and prays for us when we cannot. His yoke is easy, and His burden is light.

As you continue in your grief journey, identify verses on which to meditate. Search the Bible to discover firsthand what it has to say about grief, hope, and loss. Store God's Word in your heart for your times of need. Write key verses on a note card, and hang them in visible locations in your house. As you read them, pray the words of Scripture back to God. Ask the Lord's help to believe them and trust Him. God's Word is a rock, comfort, and healing balm to us in our grief.

On the following pages are verses to memorize.

Verses to Memorize

Identify 2-3 verses below to memorize and pray to the Lord:

- *The Spirit of the Lord God is on me, because the Lord has anointed me to bring good news to the poor. He has sent me to heal the brokenhearted, to proclaim liberty to the captives and freedom to the prisoners; to proclaim the year of the Lord's favor, and the day of our God's vengeance; to comfort all who mourn. — Isaiah 61:1-2*

- *I will never leave you or abandon you. — Hebrews 13:5*

- *Do not fear, for I have redeemed you; I have called you by your name; you are mine. I will be with you when you pass through the waters, and when you pass through the rivers, they will not overwhelm you. You will not be scorched when you walk through the fire, and the flame will not burn you. For I am the Lord your God, the Holy One of Israel, and your Savior.*
  — Isaiah 43:1-3

- *The Lord—the Lord is a compassionate and gracious God, slow to anger and abounding in faithful love and truth.*
  — Exodus 34:6

- *The Lord is good, a stronghold in a day of distress; he cares for those who take refuge in him. — Nahum 1:7*

- *Blessed be the God and Father of our Lord Jesus Christ, the Father of mercies and the God of all comfort. He comforts us in all our affliction, so that we may be able to comfort those who are in any kind of affliction, through the comfort we ourselves receive from God. For just as the sufferings of Christ overflow to us, so also through Christ our comfort overflows. — 2 Corinthians 1:3-5*

- *You planned evil against me; God planned it for good to bring about the present result—the survival of many people.*
  — Genesis 50:20

- *We know that all things work together for the good of those who love God, who are called according to his purpose.*
  — Romans 8:28

- *The God of all grace, who called you to his eternal glory in Christ, will himself restore, establish, strengthen, and support you after you have suffered a little while. To him be dominion forever. Amen.* — 1 Peter 5:10-11

> "
> WE KNOW THAT ALL THINGS WORK TOGETHER FOR THE GOOD OF THOSE WHO LOVE GOD, WHO ARE CALLED *according to His purpose*
>
> ROMANS 8:28

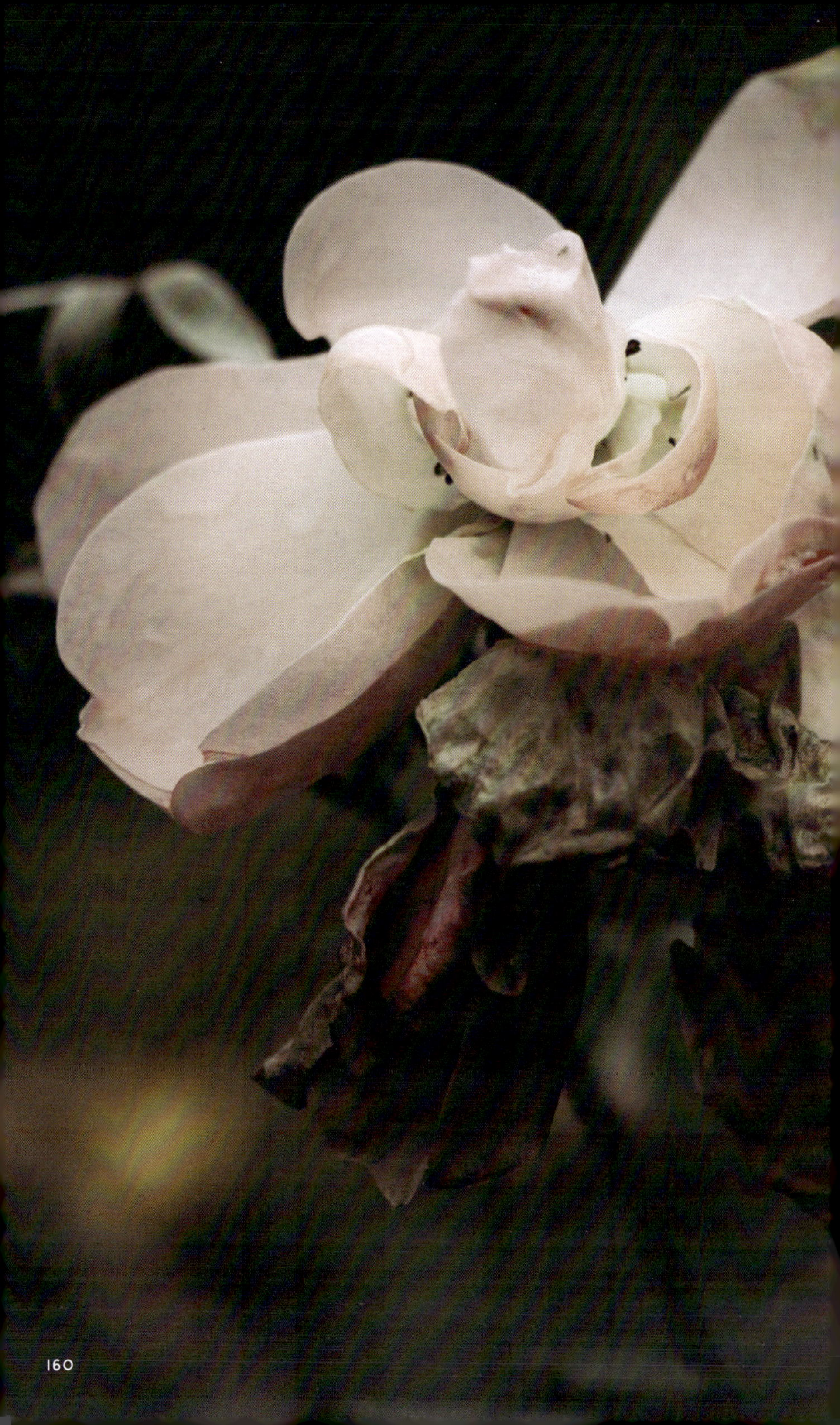

07

HELPING SOMEONE WHO IS GRIEVING

Listen
Pray
The Ministry of Presence
Acts of Service
Be Patient, Consistent, and Loving

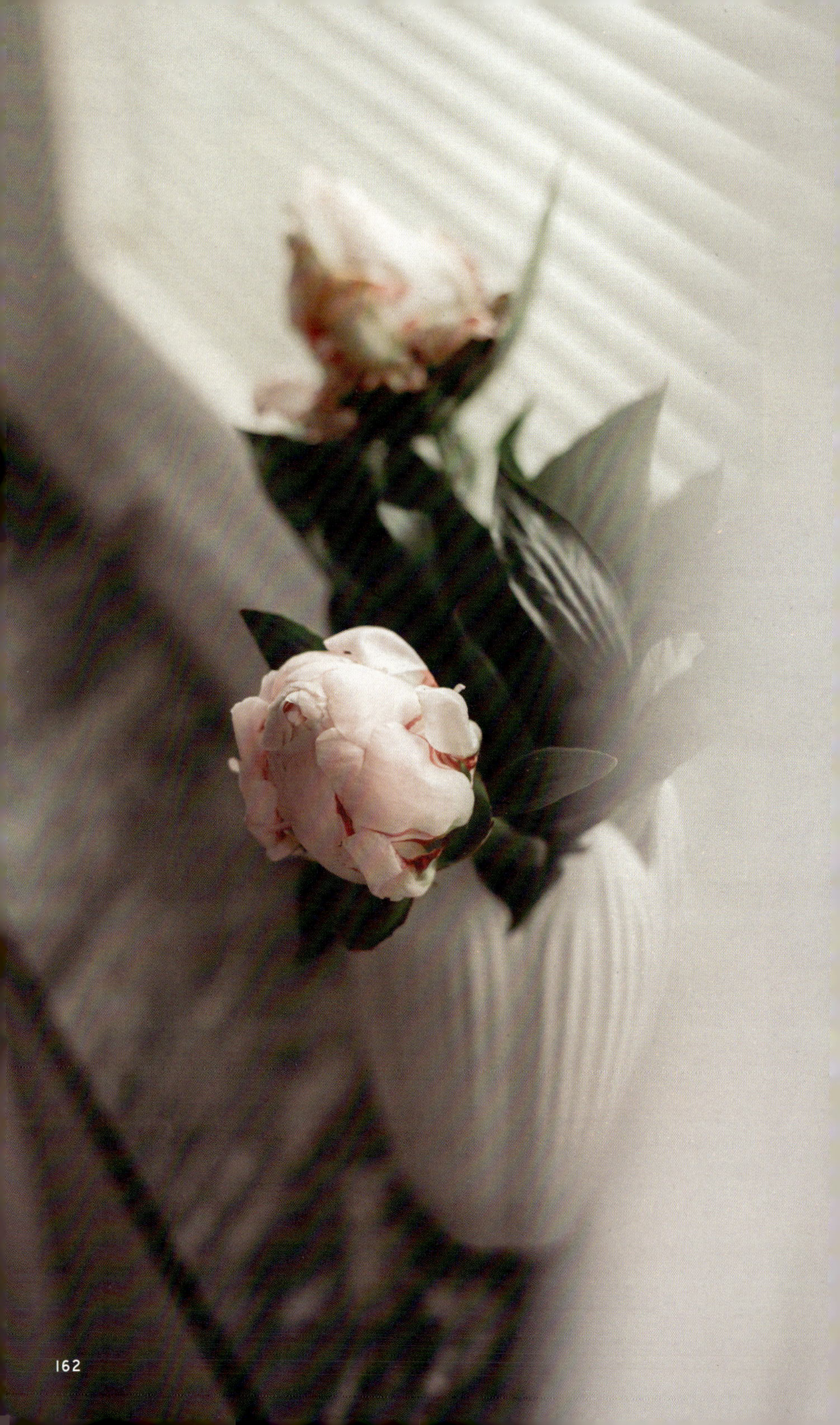

LISTEN

God calls Christians to carry the burdens of their brothers and sisters. If you are reading this booklet to better understand the grief of another, you are off to a great start. It is a commendable desire to want to help someone else in the midst of their pain.

One of the best gifts we can give to our grieving friends is to listen. Instead of trying to find the perfect things to say, you can love your friend by providing a safe space to share her thoughts. As you listen, show with your body language that you care for your friend and are interested in what she has to say. Presume that your friend is grieving, and give her the freedom to express what her grief is like.

Sometimes we do not want to follow up with those who are grieving because we do not want to make them sad. We do not want to remind them of their pain. But a grieving person is always longing for their loved one at some level. When you mention their loved one by name, you are not reminding your friend of her loss but rather giving her the opportunity to talk about what is most important to her. When you do speak, tell your friend that you are sorry for her loss. Cry with her. Express that you do not know the perfect words but that you want to be there for her. Even if your friend does not want to talk, you can offer her your prayer and a hug, along with your physical and emotional support.

On the following pages you will find questions to ask a grieving friend.

Questions to Ask a Grieving Friend

- *"Can I bring you a meal, watch your kids, or do your laundry?"*

  Try not to ask, "What can we do for you?" because it can be overwhelming for a grieving person to make decisions. Instead, offer specific help. Ask if you can bring over a meal or mow their lawn. Ask if you can watch their kids for an evening or if they want someone to talk to about their grief.

- *Do you feel like talking?*

  Do not presume that your friends want to talk, but make yourself available to them. By expressing your desire to listen, you can lovingly ask questions without forcing a conversation.

- *What is your grief like these days?*

  With good intentions, we often ask grieving people, "How are you?" Although this can be a good question, it can sometimes pressure our friends to say that they are "good" or "getting better" because they know what others want to hear. Instead, ask your friends what their grief looks like these days. Presume that your friends are grieving, and give them an opportunity to express their emotions to you.

- *What was your loved one like?*

  Mention your friend's loved one by name. Give them the opportunity to talk about their loved one, and express that you are always there to listen to stories and memories if they want to share.

- *What are some of the things you miss most about your loved one?*

  Even if you have gone through a similar loss, do not tell your friend that you know how they feel, and try not to turn the attention to yourself. While you may have similar experiences, you do not know exactly how they feel in her body with their emotions, history, and background. Provide the space for your friends to share how they are feeling.

- *Are there times in the day or year when you notice you miss your loved one most?*

  As a follow-up, reach out to your friend during the times they mention, and let them know you are praying for them.

> *One of the best gifts* we can give to our grieving friends is to listen.

── PRAY ──

We pray for someone's suffering to go away. We pray for peace and patience. We pray for the alleviation of pain. With good intentions, we pray for our hurting friend's pain to stop and for them to be happy again. But in Scripture, we find a more robust theology of suffering. We discover that God is not absent in our suffering. Rather, He uses suffering for our good, according to His divine purposes. While it is not wrong to pray that the suffering ceases, we should also remember the promises of God that He is working in all circumstances for His glory and our good (Romans 8:28).

How to Pray for Your Grieving Friend

When our friends are grieving, we can pray for:

- Faith to trust God when life hurts
- Comfort and strength
- Healing and relief from pain
- Protection
- Endurance
- Community to hold them up when their faith is weak
- Greater dependence on the Lord in prayer
- A trust in God that covers their fears
- Mental clarity in daily activities
- Wisdom in making decisions

- Opportunities to serve others
- That we can be a gospel witness to unbelieving neighbors, friends, and family members
- That God's Word would be their rock and comfort
- The ability to dwell on what is true
- Wisdom in how to love and serve our friends in their grief
- Physical health
- Emotional health
- Spiritual health

- _____
- _____
- _____
- _____
- _____

> *God is with us in our suffering*
> AND HE BEARS OUR PAINS

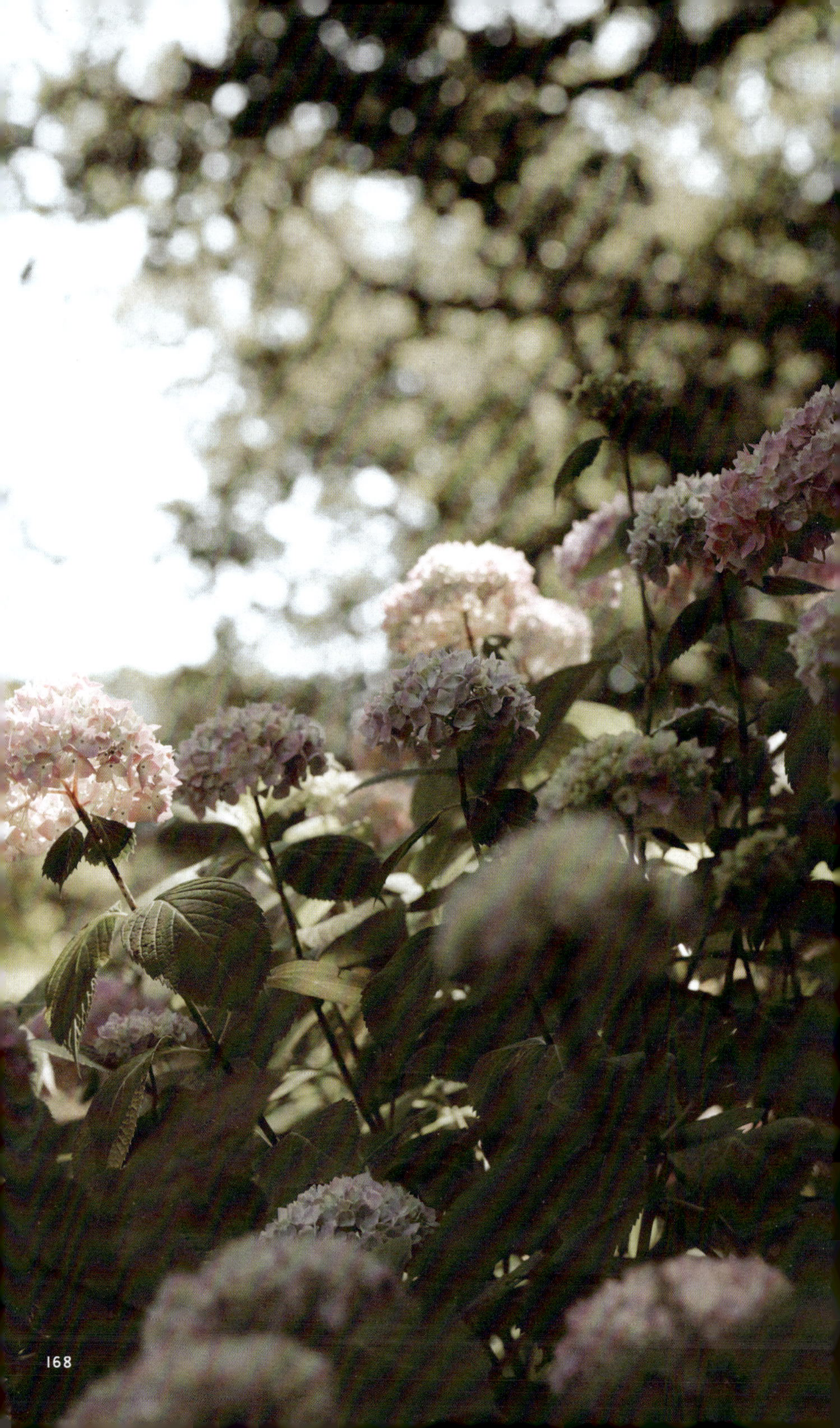

THE MINISTRY OF PRESENCE

There is power in the presence of a friend. Although it may not seem like you are doing much, make an effort to show up for your friend in their moments of grief. Show up to the funeral, and attend the visitation. Show up to the hospital with coffee, or bring flowers to their house. Show up in the moment of your friend's loss, and keep showing up in the weeks and months that follow. We can love others by being present in their moments of loss and by entering into their seasons of pain.

The power of incarnational ministry is clearly expressed in the life of Jesus. God could have saved His children from a distance, snapping His fingers or speaking a word from afar, but instead He came close. He sent His Son Jesus to enter into our pain. Jesus joined with us in the brokenness of life from His birth, being born to poor parents in a dirty stable, and wailing the cry of every newborn baby. He accumulated scrapes and aches as He grew. He felt hunger, thirst, exhaustion, and betrayal. He washed the feet of dirty sinners and befriended those who would later deny Him. He wept with those who wept and rejoiced with those who rejoiced. He ate, slept, laughed, and grieved with His friends. God is with us in our suffering, and He bears our pains. In the same way, it means a lot when you show up for your grieving friend.

Remember, when you visit your friend, you do not need to have the perfect thing to say. There is nothing that you can say that will fix their pain, and your goal is not necessarily to make them feel better. Your goal is to love them and be with them in their pain. Your friend may need to feel sad for a while, and that is okay. Sit with them, cry with them, pray with them, read Scripture over them, and offer a listening ear when they want to talk.

What Not to Say

As you comfort someone who is grieving, enter into their pain. Avoid trite platitudes, which are designed like a quick bandaid fix of a deep wound. Examples may include:

- *"I know how you feel."* – Even if you have experienced a similar loss, you do not know your friend's experience with grief. If you have experienced a similar loss, you will be able to comfort them in a unique way (2 Corinthians 1:3-11), but do not presume that their experience will be exactly the same as yours. Instead, be a good listener, and find helpful ways to serve them in their loss.

- *"At least _____"* – At least you know you can get pregnant. At least you are still young and can get remarried. At least you have your health. At least… While it is normal to want to express these kinds of platitudes, they aim to minimize someone's pain and are not helpful for someone who is grieving. It makes grieving people feel like they must look on the bright side in order to make you feel comfortable and that they cannot be honest with you about their pain.

- *Questions that serve your curiosity* – Do not ask if they did anything that merited their loss. Additionally, do not ask for the gruesome details of an accident. If your friend wants to offer these details, lovingly listen to them, but do not unnecessarily pry to satisfy your curiosity.

- *"Maybe you didn't have enough faith."* – Throughout the Scriptures, God intentionally allows lasting suffering to exist in the lives of His children. He does not promise to remove every trial, but He promises to be with us in the midst of them, using every moment of suffering for His glory and our good. To follow Christ does not mean that we will have an easy life, even if we have abundant faith.

- *"God has a plan."* – There may be a moment later on to encourage your friend about the divine purposes of God, but first aim to grieve with them. Do not try to put all the puzzle pieces together and explain why God must have allowed this loss. Be compassionate and empathetic. Listen, and ask how they are feeling. Ask how you can be praying for them.
- *"God needed her in heaven more than we needed her here."* – God does not need anything, and this comment is untrue and unhelpful. It paints an untrue and unsympathetic view of God to our grieving friends.
- *"Look on the bright side."* – In trials, it is not helpful to be told to be more positive. Instead, you can pray for your friend and encourage them with the truths of Scripture. Write them a letter filled with Scripture that you are praying for them. Help them tangibly in their day-to-day needs.
- *"You'll be fine."* – Life may not feel fine in the midst of grief, and this is an unhelpful and unsympathetic response. Instead, seek to listen to their expressions of grief and offer support and love.
- *"You are brave or strong."* – Your friend may not feel strong or brave at the moment. Instead of pointing them to a hidden inner strength, go with them to the throne of God. Pray with them, and remind them of the Lord's strength to help them in times of weakness.

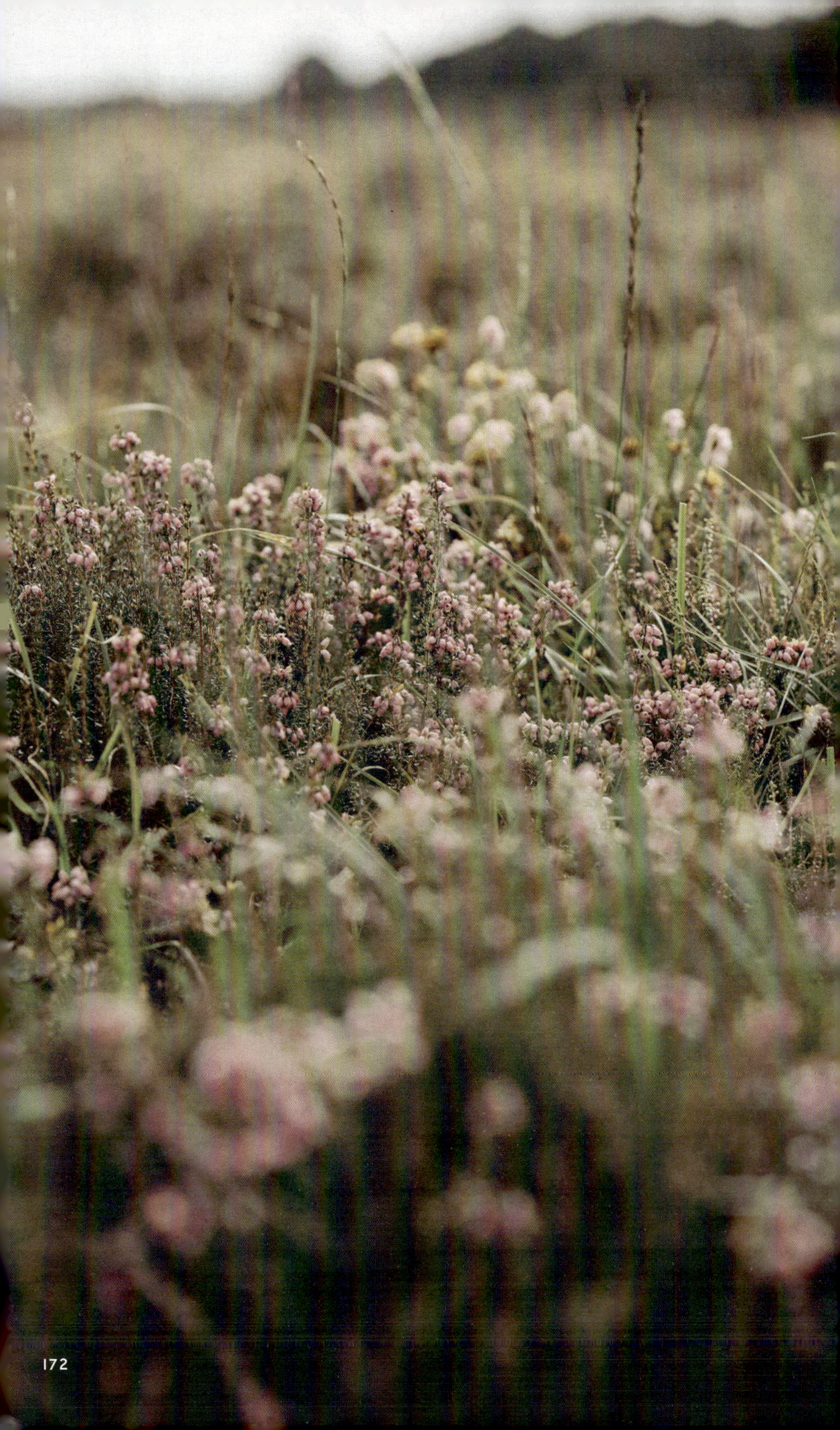

ACTS OF SERVICE

As you read about the physical effects of grief in this booklet, notice how disruptive they can be to everyday life. Imagine how simple tasks—like mowing the yard or going to the doctor—can become seemingly insurmountable in the face of grief.

To love your friend, find ways to help them in their day-to-day lives. They may not know how to ask for help or even what help they need. So instead of asking the question, "How can I help?", offer tangible suggestions. Depending on your relational capital, you may be able to take the initiative to help in ways you know they need. Perhaps you can mow their yard and quietly leave a note saying that you love them. Or you can send a card in the mail with the ways that you are praying for them, drop off a gift card for groceries, or offer to treat them to dinner. Maybe you can create a meal chain to include your church members or organize childcare as needed.

As we serve those around us, we become the hands and feet of Christ to our friends. On the following page, make a list of actions that would be helpful to your specific friend. If possible, involve your community in accomplishing these items.

Ideas for Serving Your Grieving Friends

- Cook a meal.
- Give a gift card for groceries.
- Organize a sign-up list for others interested in providing meals.
- Help with logistics, as able. (Ideas may include offering help to find a funeral home, communicating with loved ones about recent developments, etc.)

- Help with their resumé if they are applying for jobs.
- Show up to mow their lawn, rake leaves, or shovel their driveway.
- Help find a biblical counselor.
- Help find a trusted doctor.
- Bring them vitamins with a note that reads something like, "I know this season is incredibly difficult. Your body is probably under a lot of stress these days, so here are some vitamins to help boost your immune system. We love you and are praying for you."
- Write Scripture on a card, and mail it to them with a note saying, "Praying these verses over you today. We love you."
- Listen to your friend if he or she wants to talk.
- Text your friend to let them know you are praying for them.
- Offer to take his or her kids to the park for a few hours or provide childcare as needed.

> ❝
> AS WE SERVE THOSE AROUND US, WE BECOME *the hands and feet of Christ* TO OUR FRIENDS

Helping Your Grieving Friend

Use the following section to brainstorm how to help your friend in their specific season of grief

-
-
-
-
-
-
-
-
-
-
-
-
-
-

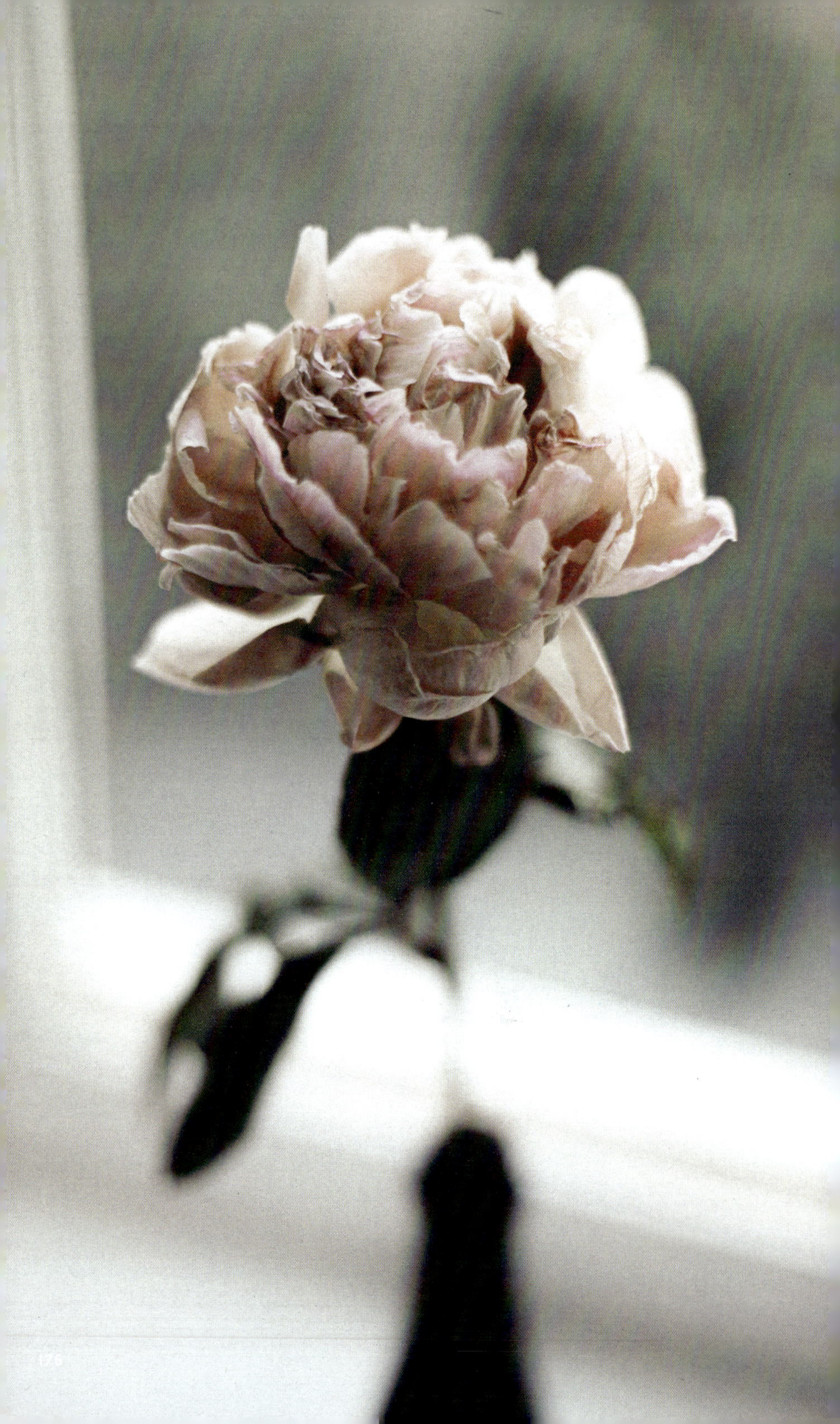

Be Patient, Consistent, and Loving

As you love your friend, put their needs above your own. Be patient, consistent, and loving.

Be Patient

When those around us are in pain, we want to fix it. We want to help take away their pain and ease their burdens. In our attempts to bring comfort, we often jump in with a myriad of quick solutions. More selfishly, at times, the prolonged pain of another may make us uncomfortable or become inconvenient to us. We want our friend to get better so that life can go back to how it was before. Healing from loss takes time, so be patient with your friend in their grief journey. Consider ways to serve your friend, and follow up with them months after the loss. Write down important dates (date of death, anniversary, important markers, etc.), so you can check in with your friend. Though it may seem like the world has moved on, it is a comfort to talk about their loss with trusted friends.

As your friend grieves, you may also experience loss of your own. You may miss your friend—who they were or the laughter that once came so easily between you. You may miss your weekly movie nights or the conversation that flowed so naturally. As you are patient with your friend's grief journey, consider your own loss, and turn to the Lord for help, as expressed in the first sections of this booklet.

Be Consistent

As a response to grief, your friend's emotions may fluctuate. They may be angry one moment and sad the next. As much as possible, be a stable, consistent presence of love in their lives. Point them to the constant love of Christ, and keep showing up for them in their pain.

Be Loving

When we love those around us, we commit to entering into the pain of another and put their needs above our own. We willingly pour our time, energy, and emotions into our hurting friends as we enter into their difficult seasons. We love them in word and deed, crying with them and praying for them. Though it may be a difficult season, continue to love your friend in word and deed. Be a listening ear, offer tangible support, and ask about how they are grieving. In doing so, you are showing Christ's love to them.

What to Say to a Grieving Friend

- Say something. Sometimes we do not want to say the wrong thing, so we say nothing at all. But when we do not acknowledge someone's loss, it can feel to our friend like we do not want to talk about the most important thing in their life.

- "My heart is hurting for you."

- "I miss her too" or "I remember…" If you knew their loved one, mention him or her with specific stories. Keep saying the name of the person who died.

- Write down stories of their loved one, so they can read it later.

- On important dates (birthdays, anniversaries, etc), send them a message that you are thinking of your friend and praying for them.

- "What was she like? I want you to know I'm here just to listen, if you ever want to talk about them."

If you did not know their loved one, ask about them by name. Be a good listener, and offer to be a sounding board for any stories, questions, or general processing of their emotions.

- "I have never been through what you are going through, but I want to walk alongside you in your grief. I am here for you."

- Hurt with them. Agree that this is the worst.

- "What is your grief like these days?" Give your friend the opportunity to express his or her grief. Do not assume that you know what they are feeling or judge them for their emotions. Rather, let them express how they are feeling.

- Follow your friend's lead about what he or she wants to talk about.

- Be okay with empty space in conversations. It is not your job to say the perfect thing but to sit with them in their grief and enter into their pain. If you do, it is more likely they will come to you in the future. Listen as if you are taking prayer requests, not to fix it.

- "No one has the words that would remove your pain, but so many wish they did."

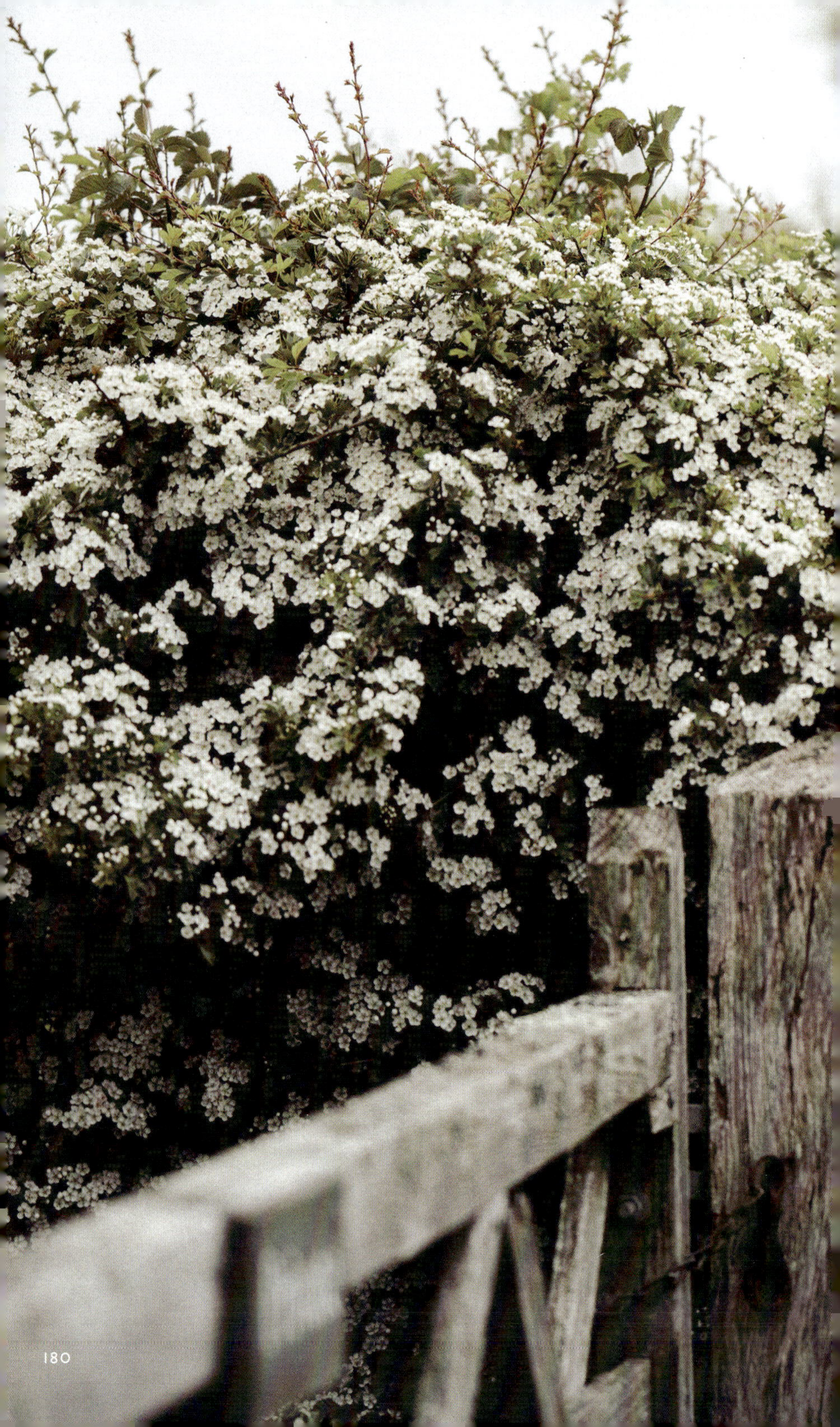

—08—

GOD IN OUR GRIEF

He is with Us
He Weeps with Us
He Redeems Your Suffering

HE IS WITH US

God is with us in our grief. He does not abandon us in our moments of sorrow but surrounds us with His love. He cares for us when we are weak and provides for us when we are needy (Matthew 6:25-34). He heals our broken hearts and bandages our wounds (Psalm 147:3). He does not withdraw from us in our pain; He is with us in it. Though it may be hard to see God through our pain, we can trust in faith that He is here. He is simultaneously reigning on His throne, competently ruling over all and tenderly holding us through every moment of sorrow.

Our loss of loved ones, dreams, and desires remind us that while God is with us, His work is not yet finished. He is still actively working, loving, and redeeming all things. He loves us fully with a steadfast, faithful, and all-sufficient love. Every time someone dies, it reminds us that God's work is not yet finished. He is coming to redeem all things and will not leave this world broken. Though we cannot yet see God clearly, our grief reminds us that He is at work. He is actively restoring the broken and healing the hurt. The God of angel armies is with us, our help, King, Lord, and friend. He is with us today, and He promises to one day make all things new (Revelation 21:5).

As we grow in our love for God, we begin to see how beautiful, awesome, holy, and perfect He is. Our awareness of His surpassing greatness expands with our growing faith, and we begin to want God even more than we want relief from suffering. We discover that He is our surpassing joy, love, peace, and hope. The God who is perfectly good, wise, kind, and just — this God is with us. He reigns over all, and He is enough to satisfy every longing of our weary hearts.

HOW FIRM A FOUNDATION

How firm a foundation, ye saints of the Lord,
Is laid for your faith in His excellent word!
What more can He say than to you He hath said,
To you who for refuge to Jesus have fled?

Fear not, I am with thee, O be not dismayed,
For I am thy God, and will still give thee aid;
I'll strengthen thee, help thee, and cause thee to stand,
Upheld by My righteous, omnipotent hand.

When through the deep waters I call thee to go,
The rivers of sorrow shall not overflow;
For I will be with thee, thy troubles to bless,
And sanctify to thee thy deepest distress.

When through fiery trials thy pathway shall lie,
My grace, all sufficient, shall be thy supply;
The flame shall not hurt thee; I only design
Thy dross to consume, and thy gold to refine.

E'en down to old age all My people shall prove
My sovereign, eternal, unchangeable love;
And then, when grey hairs shall their temples adorn,
Like lambs they shall still in My bosom be borne.

The soul that on Jesus hath leaned for repose,
I will not, I will not desert to his foes;
That soul, though all hell should endeavor to shake,
I'll never, no, never, no, never forsake!

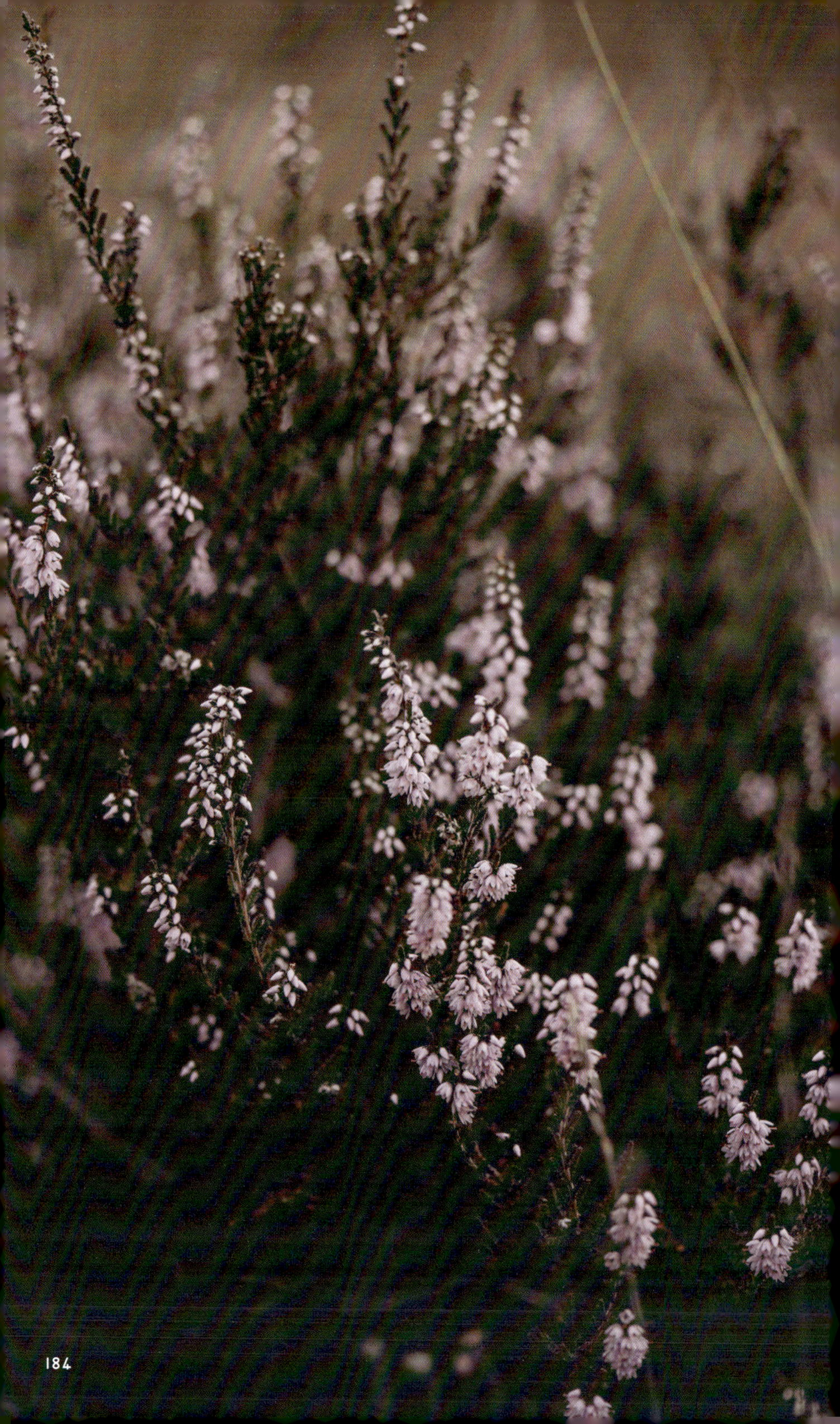

HE WEEPS WITH US

God weeps with us. He understands our pain and knows our sorrows. Because Jesus pierced His human feet on the rocky roads of earth, enduring pain and experiencing loss, we know that He empathizes with us in our grief. This is the hope of the incarnation—that though fully God, holy and majestic in every way, Christ entered into our pain. As Jesus was born on earth, fully God and fully man, He experienced hardship. He was rejected by men and acquainted with grief (Isaiah 53:3). He went hungry and thirsty and grieved over the brokenness of the world (John 11:17-37). He endured the shame of a criminal's execution and was abandoned by God on a rugged cross, bearing our sins so that we no longer have to carry their weight. Truly, He understands the grief and sorrow of life, having experienced it firsthand. Because of this, we know that we have a Great High Priest who sympathizes with us in our weakness (Hebrews 4:15). We have a Savior, Jesus, who knows what it means to be forsaken, betrayed, and alone. He does not condemn us as we cry but rather comes close and draws us into Himself.

Even though Jesus has the power to erase every wound, He still chooses to enter into our pain with us. When His friend, Lazarus, died in John 11, Jesus wept with His friends, even though He knew He would raise Lazarus from the dead moments later. If we slow down to consider this, Jesus's tears are remarkable evidence of His tender love. God did not withdraw from His people, even for a second. He entered into their grief and loss because He is perfect in love. In the same way, Jesus does not close His heart to us, even for a second. He enters into every moment of our pain as One who loves us and who understands our grief.

God is not only with us in our tears, but He also weeps with us. He knows every tear we cry and keeps them carefully counted in a bottle (Psalm 56:8). He is tender-hearted toward us, as a loving and compassionate Father. So, when tears blur your vision and you cannot think past tomorrow, when you feel heavy-laden and overwhelmed by the aches of loss, fall on Christ. Come to Him, and find rest for your souls. His yoke is easy, and His burden is light (Matthew 11:28-30). He is with you in your sadness. He empathizes with you, and He feels your pain. He does not rush you along in your tears or pain, but He is patient with you in it, as a loving and faithful friend.

> **GOD IS NOT ONLY WITH US IN OUR TEARS, BUT HE** *also weeps with us*

MAN OF SORROWS

*Man of sorrows what a name
for the Son of God, who came
ruined sinners to reclaim:
Hallelujah, what a Savior!*

*Bearing shame and scoffing rude,
in my place condemned he stood,
sealed my pardon with his blood:
Hallelujah, what a Savior!*

*Guilty, helpless, lost were we;
blameless Lamb of God was he,
sacrificed to set us free:
Hallelujah, what a Savior!*

*He was lifted up to die;
"It is finished" was his cry;
now in heaven exalted high:
Hallelujah, what a Savior!*

*When he comes, our glorious King,
all his ransomed home to bring,
then anew this song we'll sing:
Hallelujah, what a Savior!*

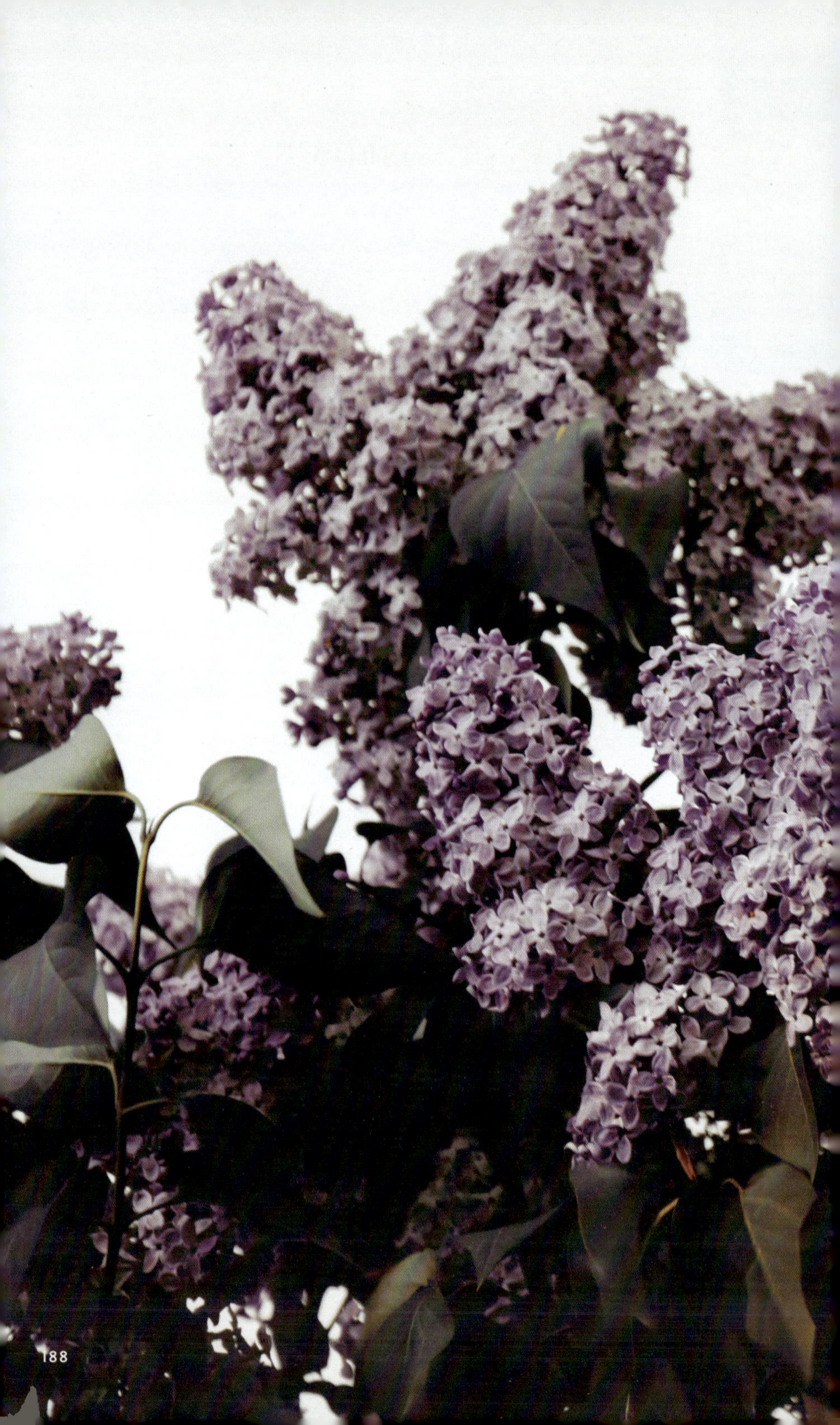

HE REDEEMS YOUR SUFFERING

God is doing something in your suffering. Even though the night may feel dark, Scripture tells us that God is working for our good in the midst of darkness. He promises to redeem every ounce of our suffering for His glory and our good (Romans 8:28). He promises to bring good out of evil (Genesis 50:20), to heal broken hearts, and bandage gaping wounds (Psalm 147:3). He promises to redeem and work good out of suffering (Romans 5:3-4).

God will not waste a moment of your sorrow. In the midst of suffering, He will change your priorities and perspectives. He may strengthen your prayers and redirect your affections toward Him. He may grow your eternal perspective and teach you to count your days so that you have a heart of wisdom (Psalm 90:12). He will teach you to trust Him. Though we may not be able to see it right away, we can trust in the good and faithful character of God. Our suffering is not meaningless.

God's redemption is seen most clearly in the life, death, and resurrection of His Son. When Jesus was killed that dreadful Friday, the world was dark. There seemed to be no hope. Even His followers could not understand how there could be a grander purpose in this suffering. Yet, through death, God was weaving a grander story of redemption. Through this heinous injustice, the death and condemnation of an innocent man, God was saving His children and creating resurrection hope for all who would trust in Him.

Because of the cross, we can have hope today. Although we may be tempted to give up hope because of our grief, we press on in faith. As Paul says, "Therefore we do not give up. Even though our outer person is being destroyed, our inner person is being renewed day by day. For our momentary light affliction is producing for us an absolutely incomparable eternal weight of glory. So we do not focus on what is seen but on what is unseen. For what is seen is temporary, but what is unseen is eternal" (2 Corinthians 4:16-18). His power, goodness, and redemption are not too good to be true. He is our living hope and will somehow, miraculously, work for our good, even out of our suffering and sorrow. We can trust our Savior that our pain and trials are not in vain. He will grow us in ways we cannot even imagine.

> *We can trust our Savior*
> **THAT OUR PAIN AND TRIALS ARE NOT IN VAIN**

HE WILL HOLD ME FAST

When I fear my faith will fail,
Christ will hold me fast;
When the tempter would prevail,
He can hold me fast!

REFRAIN
He will hold me fast,
He will hold me fast;
For my Savior loves me so,
He will hold me fast.

I could never keep my hold,
He must hold me fast;
For my love is often cold,
He must hold me fast. [Refrain]

I am precious in His sight,
He will hold me fast;
Those He saves are His delight,
He will hold me fast. [Refrain]

He'll not let my soul be lost,
Christ will hold me fast;
Bought by Him at such a cost,
He will hold me fast. [Refrain]

Amen.

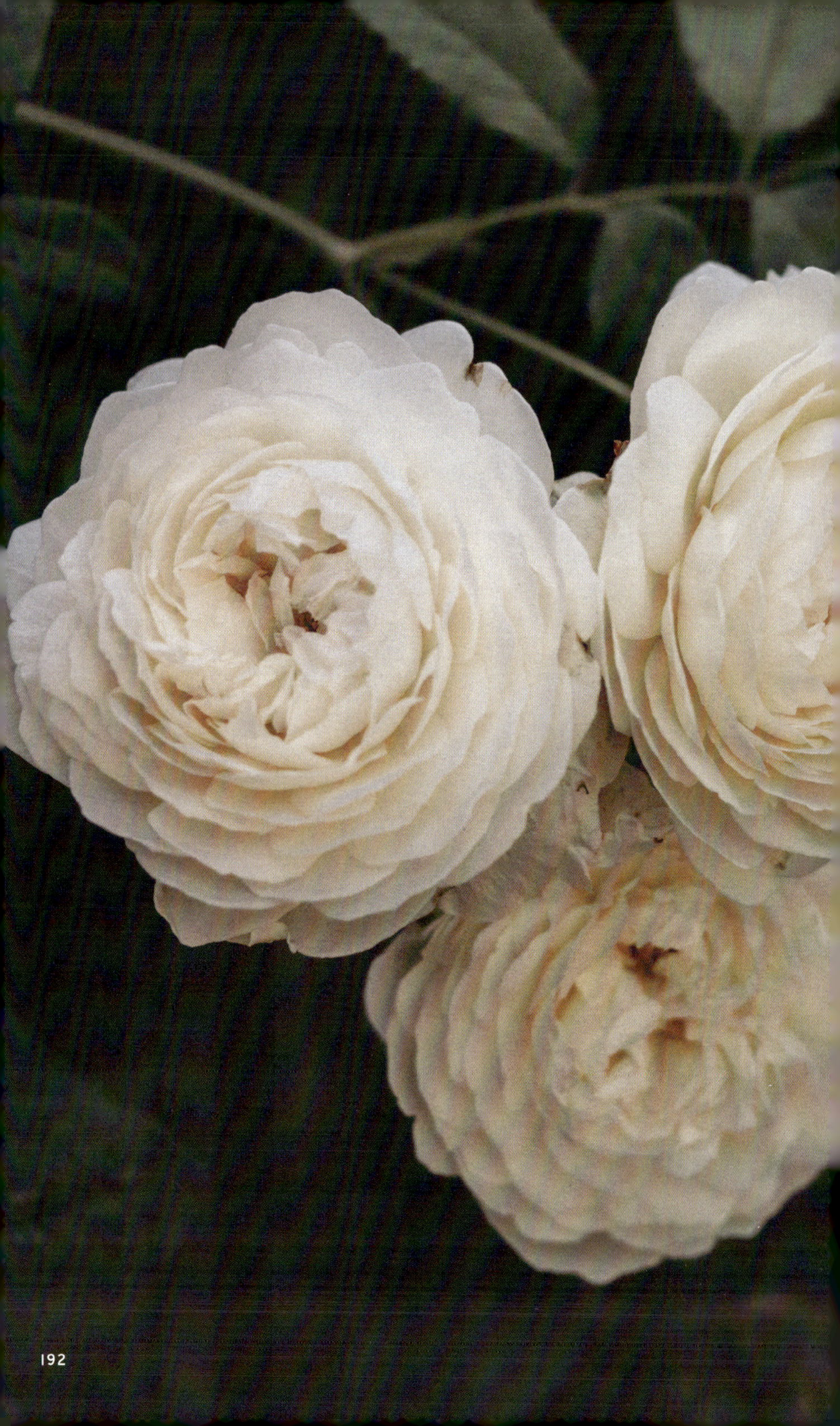

09

THE FUTURE OF GRIEF

Healing is a process of both holding on and letting go. As you seek God in the midst of your grief, He will begin to heal you. In time, your grief will begin to fade. Your fatigue will lift. Your pain will not consume you anymore. You will be able to make decisions again, eat balanced meals, and look forward to holidays again. You will be able to focus on your reading and find reasons to be thankful.

At times, we can postpone healing because our pain helps us feel close to the one we lost. Healing can feel dishonoring to the memory of our loved one. But when the pain begins to subside and you can dream again about tomorrow, it does not mean that you do not cherish the one you have lost or do not still mourn their loss. Rather, it is a form of healing with a scar. Because of your grief, you will be different. Your life will never be the same, and you may walk through the rest of your life with an invisible limp. But through each step, you will find that God is your faithful and present help. He is with you to help you and strengthen you in this new normal. He will grow your compassion and love for others. And one day, He will return to make all things new and right every wrong.

Our grief reminds us that this world is broken. We are in need of a Savior—One who will repair all the jagged, painful pieces of life. And one day, God promises to do just that. He will return to right every injustice and heal every hurt. In the new heaven and the new earth, there will be no more crying, pain, or death. We will be full and complete in Christ, filled with indescribable joy.

As we close this study, find hope in the day that is to come, when Jesus returns to make all things right:

> *Then I saw a new heaven and a new earth; for the first heaven and the first earth had passed away, and the sea was no more. I also saw the holy city, the new Jerusalem, coming down out of heaven from God, prepared like a bride adorned for her husband. Then I*

heard a loud voice from the throne: Look, God's dwelling is with humanity, and he will live with them. They will be his peoples, and God himself will be with them and will be their God. He will wipe away every tear from their eyes. Death will be no more; grief, crying, and pain will be no more, because the previous things have passed away. Then the one seated on the throne said, "Look, I am making everything new." — Revelation 21:1-5

Though our sorrow may last for the night, joy will come in the morning (Psalm 30:5). He will restore every injustice and wipe every tear. He is good, and all He does is good. So together we pray, "Lord, come soon."

A MIGHTY FORTRESS IS OUR GOD

A mighty fortress is our God, a bulwark never failing; our helper he, amid the flood of mortal ills prevailing. For still our ancient foe does seek to work us woe; his craft and power are great, and armed with cruel hate, on earth is not his equal.

Did we in our own strength confide, our striving would be losing, were not the right Man on our side, the Man of God's own choosing. You ask who that may be? Christ Jesus, it is he; Lord Sabaoth his name, from age to age the same; and he must win the battle.

And though this world, with devils filled, should threaten to undo us, we will not fear, for God has willed his truth to triumph through us. The prince of darkness grim, we tremble not for him; his rage we can endure, for lo! his doom is sure; one little word shall fell him.

That Word above all earthly powers no thanks to them abideth; the Spirit and the gifts are ours through him who with us sideth. Let goods and kindred go, this mortal life also; the body they may kill: God's truth abideth still; his kingdom is forever!

PSALM 46

*God is our refuge and strength,
a helper who is always found
in times of trouble.
Therefore we will not be afraid,
though the earth trembles
and the mountains topple
into the depths of the seas,
though its water roars and foams
and the mountains quake with its turmoil.*

*There is a river —
its streams delight the city of God,
the holy dwelling place of the Most High.
God is within her; she will not be toppled.
God will help her when the morning dawns.
Nations rage, kingdoms topple;
the earth melts when he lifts his voice.
The Lord of Armies is with us;
the God of Jacob is our stronghold.*

*Come, see the works of the Lord,
who brings devastation on the earth.
He makes wars cease throughout the earth.
He shatters bows and cuts spears to pieces;
he sets wagons ablaze.*

*"Stop fighting, and know that I am God,
exalted among the nations, exalted on the earth."
The Lord of Armies is with us;
the God of Jacob is our stronghold.*

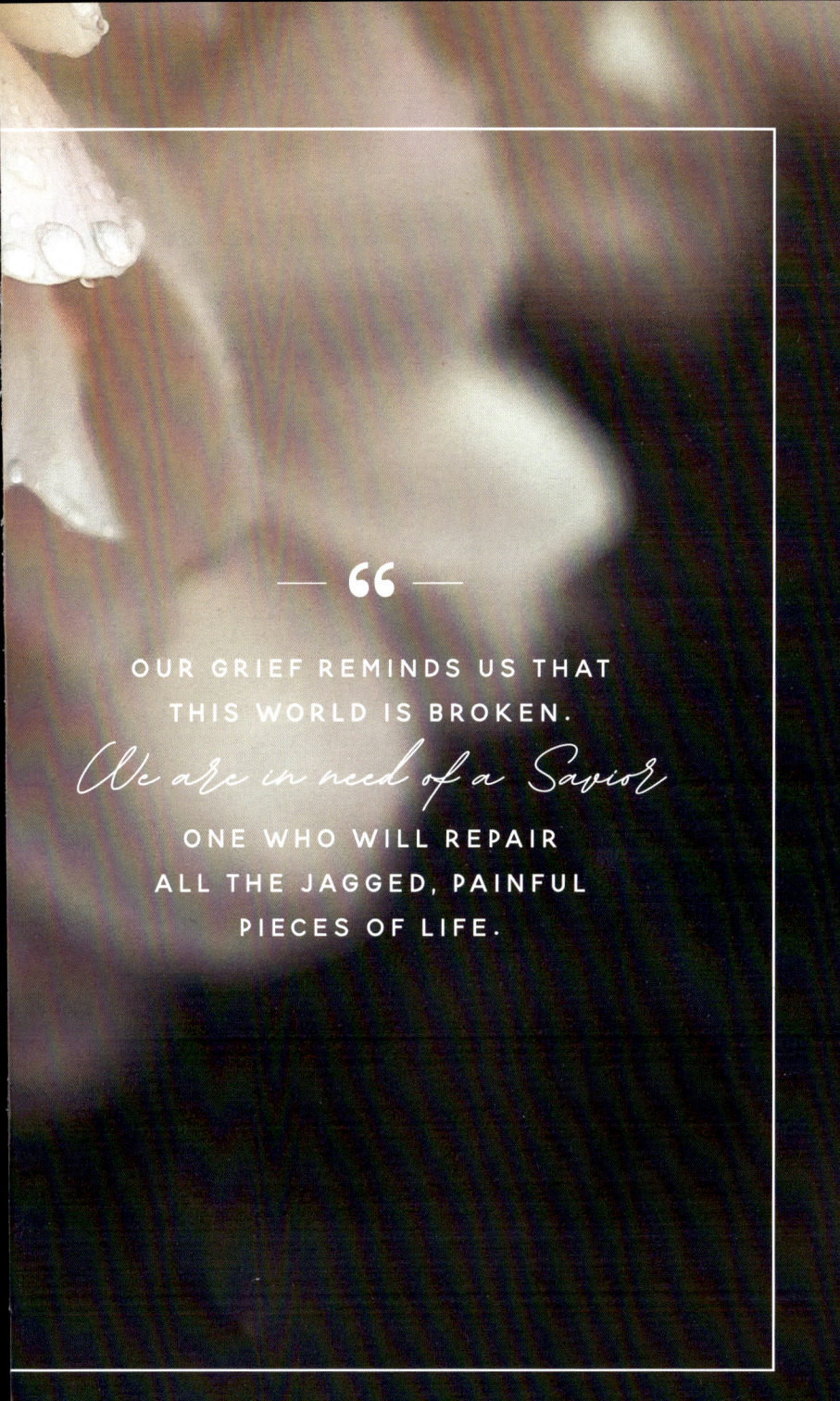

> OUR GRIEF REMINDS US THAT
> THIS WORLD IS BROKEN.
> *We are in need of a Savior,*
> ONE WHO WILL REPAIR
> ALL THE JAGGED, PAINFUL
> PIECES OF LIFE.

Thank you for studying
God's Word with us.

CONNECT WITH US

@thedailygraceco
@dailygracepodcast

CONTACT US

info@thedailygraceco.com

SHARE

#thedailygraceco

VISIT US ONLINE

www.thedailygraceco.com

MORE DAILY GRACE

The Daily Grace App
Daily Grace Podcast